Getting Into the System

of related interest

Working with Schizophrenia
A Needs Based Approach
Gwen Howe
ISBN 1 85302 242 X

LIVING WITH SERIOUS MENTAL ILLNESS 1

Getting Into the System

Gwen Howe

Jessica Kingsley Publishers
London and Philadelphia

First published in the United Kingdom in 1998 by
Jessica Kingsley Publishers Ltd
116 Pentonville Road
London N1 9JB, England
and
1900 Frost Road, Suite 101
Bristol, PA 19007, U S A

Copyright © 1998 Gwen Howe

Library of Congress Cataloging in Publication Data
A CIP catalogue record for this book is available
from the Library of Congress

British Library Cataloguing in Publication Data

Howe, Gwen
Getting into the system. – (Living with serious mental illness ; 1)
1.Mental illness – Popular works 2.Mental illness – Treatment 3.Mentally ill
– Services for
I.Title
362.2'0425

ISBN 1 85302 457 0

Printed and Bound in Great Britain by
Athenaeum Press, Gateshead, Tyne and Wear

Contents

PREFACE   7

1. Getting into the system: an introduction   11

2. Having a diagnosis and not being told   15

3. The pain of not knowing what is wrong   28

4. Teetering on the edge of the system   43

5. Juvenile sufferers: a special case   58

6. Another young sufferer slipping in
   and out of the system   73

7. Into the system, yet falling by the wayside   88

8. Getting appropriate treatment and care: a lottery? 101

9. Getting into the system: summing up   118

GLOSSARY   125
FURTHER READING   130
USEFUL ADDRESSES   132
SUBJECT INDEX   134
NAME INDEX   138

This book is dedicated to Bella Faulkner and Betty McMeekin: two of the finest nurses we know.

A note on royalties
Forty per cent of any royalties from this book will be shared between the Manic Depression Fellowship and a local group of the National Schizophrenia Fellowship.

Preface

At a time when those who work with serious mental illness are being encouraged to listen more keenly to sufferers and carers, the *Living with Serious Mental Illness* series provides an impressive opportunity for the consumer to speak and to be heard.

About the LEAP group

At the time of writing, the group is made up of eleven members. Of these, five have personal experience of manic depression (MD) or schizophrenia. The other six are close relatives of a sufferer and one of these relatives has also suffered with a depressive illness.

More about the group's members

As a matter of interest, members of the group, whose ages range from 31 to 65 years, come from very diverse backgrounds and, to a quite remarkable extent, they represent virtually the whole gamut of income levels throughout our society. Four of the group have honours degrees to their credit and one has a recent masters degree as well. One member runs her own business, having previously been a director of an old established London firm, while two regard themselves as 'ordinary housewives and mothers', despite holding down part-time jobs, supporting a mentally ill relative and doing regular voluntary work in their spare time! Two of those members who have survived a psychotic illness have responsible managerial jobs, three have experience of working with the seriously mentally ill and one of these is a trained mental health professional. Finally, all five have been been involved to a greater or lesser extent in speaking in public about their experiences and most of the relatives have taken part in professionals' training programmes.

The role of the group

In each book, the LEAP group is responsible for providing the input which appears under the headings GROUP'S ANALYSIS OF CASE STUDY and THE WIDER PERSPECTIVE and this is collected in the following ways:

1. by members completing questionnaires sent out with each draft case study, while adding as much comment and information as they feel to be relevant.

2. from discussion at regular group meetings, each dedicated to a particular case study

On average, during the compiling of the first book of the series, two thirds of the group's members have attended the meetings (with all members attending at least two of them) and three quarters of the members have regularly completed questionnaires on case studies.

In addition, the contract between members of the group and myself allows for the group's Chair, who has personal experience of a serious mental illness, and at least one other member to read and edit each chapter and for two further members to read and edit the complete book prior to its going to the publisher. It also allows for any member of the group to read and comment on any chapter at any time.

The structure of each book

Each book has a similar format. The first and last chapters take the form of an **introduction** and a **summing up** by the author. The intervening chapters focus on separate case studies, each dealing with one aspect of one individual's experience of 'the system'. The last of these chapters is devoted to five shorter case studies to broaden the scope of the experience covered in each book.

The structure of each of the chapters focusing on a case study

These chapters are made up of a **case study** and a short **comment** which includes a pause for thought and an informal exercise. This is followed by the **group's analysis of the case study** and its discussion of **the wider perspective**. The chapter ends with a short **summing up**, relevant **information** and an **exercise**. Bracketed numbers in individual chapters refer to their respective information sheets.

Under the heading **comment**, it has been assumed that readers may be interested in critically examining what is happening in individual case studies, perhaps with the help of an informal exercise, before going on to read the LEAP group's findings. This could be achieved within a group training context or, equally well, by working on one's own and making appropriate notes before proceeding with the rest of the chapter.

Under the heading **information**, references and extra information are provided which tie up with matters highlighted in the LEAP group's analysis and further discussion. There may be some repetition throughout the book, to save the need for cross referencing and to ensure that each chapter is complete in itself for reference and for training purposes.

Under the heading **exercise**, a project is proposed which is suitable for use in a group training context or as a formal piece of written work.

Case studies

The subject of each case study may be a member of the LEAP group, or a relative, friend or acquaintance of a member. It is important to point out that group members come from several different geographical areas and members are involved nationally and regionally in the voluntary sector. Thus case studies are drawn from a nationwide sample. Because of this diverse experience within the group, we are assured that consumers have remarkably similar experiences throughout England and Wales.

Please note that names and other details which are irrelevant to the basic facts of each case have been changed to protect the identity of sufferers (whether or not they are happy to 'go public'), their families and involved service providers.

What's in a name?

As I have mentioned in Introductions to my previous books, it a problem for an author to know how best to refer to individuals who have to cope with the condition which is the subject of their book and also how to refer to those most involved with these individuals. For some, this is an important issue but it is also one on which there is little agreement. Until this situation resolves itself, I hope readers will continue to bear with me while I use the terms 'sufferers' and 'carers' in the interests of expediency and a readable writing style.

Members of the LEAP Group have had similar difficulties deciding what to call themselves for the purposes of this series. Several of those who might in other circumstances be labelled with the fashionable word 'user' were adamantly against this and, in the context of their involvement in this series, there was little enthusiasm for the word 'sufferer' either. They eventually settled for the word 'survivor', acknowledging that lots of individuals like themselves are fortunate enough to find ways of largely coping with, and surviving, a serious mental illness.

Similarly, those members of the group who are relatives of individuals having to cope with a serious mental illness were not too sure about the word 'carer' as they not only feel that the word is abused by 'the system', but they also find it rather patronising. In the event, and like others before them, they nevertheless opted for the term 'carer' for the sake of convenience and clarity and nothing better coming to mind.

A message for professionals working with serious mental illness

LEAP group members have asked me to point out that as they are campaigning for better services for everyone who has to cope with a psychotic illness, it is essential that they highlight where things can and do go wrong. They would not wish this in any way to detract from the splendid work of some caring and dedicated professionals out there whose untiring efforts enable sufferers to get on with their lives successfully. LEAP group suspects that these professionals are the same ones who will be most interested in reading a series like this although it does not allow for more than a passing comment on their invaluable contribution to a deserving, but neglected, cause. The group would like to take this opportunity of saying a special 'thank you' on behalf of those sufferers who have received the sort of treatment and care which has freed them to get on with the rest of their lives despite a serious mental illness.

Finally, members of the LEAP group may be available occasionally to take part in training programmes for professionals and other mental health workers. Enquiries should be sent to me, with SAE please, care of our publishers.   *Gwen Howe, May 1997*

CHAPTER I

Getting into the system
An introduction

Serious mental illness is the name we give to conditions such as manic depression (MD) and schizophrenia. We use the word 'serious' (although sufferers can be relatively well much of the time) because at times of breakdown they can lose touch with reality. This is called a *psychotic* episode. Psychosis is dangerous because sufferers are no longer able to understand what is happening around them and, in particular, have no awareness that they are ill and in need of help. At this point, often terrified and paranoid, it is vital that they are protected from themselves and from any immediate dangers. They also need protecting from the ravages of an untreated psychosis, which can inflict irreversible damage to their health and, at worst, lead into an intractable chronic illness.

As psychosis is eminently treatable, it follows that all our efforts in the handling of serious mental illness should focus on providing (a) early acknowledgement, diagnosis and treatment of a first episode of illness, (b) full explanations about all aspects of the illness and ways of coping with it for families (and as the illness abates, the sufferer) (c) advice on ways to decrease, as far as possible, the chances of further breakdown, and (d) a 'lifeline' for sufferers and families to use if they do see signs of relapse later on, so that they can obtain an immediate response from the system.

Strangely, it seems that we don't focus our efforts in this way at present. For example, just to take point (a), far too many sufferers fall at the first hurdle and have to endure long delays in 'getting into the system'.

Prolonged delays

For many families, the worst time in a serious mental illness is when they are waiting for acknowledgement that something is wrong with their relative. They speak of turning to doctors and other professionals for help and coming back empty-handed, to the anguish of watching a loved one become a stranger in front of their eyes. When help eventually arrives – often in a crisis which demands urgent action by mental health professionals or, quite frequently, the police – they describe their experience of trying in vain to get professionals to listen to them as 'having been to hell and back'.

A nightmare

This is the stuff that nightmares are made of, but, make no mistake about it, it can be very much a reality for those trying to obtain help for someone developing a serious mental illness. For example, Johnstone and colleagues (1986) found in their study of 462 first episodes of schizophrenia that the interval between onset of illness and admission varied widely, but was often more than one year and associated with severe behavioural disturbance and family difficulty in arranging appropriate care. These workers concluded that their findings 'allowed no interpretation other than that appropriate services were not available to these people when they were required'.[1]

Relatives continue to report that delays can go on for long after they, their friends and their neighbours have come to the conclusion that the individual must be mentally ill. Sadly, this means that the sufferer will by then have gained a reputation which could have been avoided, particularly if the illness turns out to be eminently treatable, as is often the case.

But why?

In short, for all sorts of reasons the working of the system makes it very likely that professionals will stand back and wait for a crisis to erupt

[1]   Johnstone, E.C. *et al.* (1986) The Northwick Park Study of First Episodes of Schizophrenia, Part I: 'Presentation of the Illness and Problems Relating to Admission', *British Journal of Psychiatry*, 148, 115–120.

before intervening in a new case of serious mental illness and sometimes in later relapses too. The reasons for this are complicated[2] and have less to do with a 'right to treatment and care' than with political expendiency and ideologies originating in the 1960s. They also have a lot to do with 'labelling theories' and a reluctance to label someone with a condition surrounded by stigma (although, as we have just noted, delays in obtaining a diagnosis and appropriate treatment can actually achieve this all on their own).

Moreover, concerns with 'labelling', stigma and civil rights are not even relevant if a developing psychosis is caught early enough, at a time when the individual is still aware enough to accept help and treatment. However, because of 'the system's' pronounced tendency to avoid acknowledging that something is wrong, this often doesn't happen. Instead, the psychosis becomes entrenched and the individual loses touch with reality. At this stage, there may be a need to resort to the law, and then all the other factors touched on above come into play, often causing further delay rather than facilitating diagnosis and treatment.

Early treatment and care: a priority

When it was decided to produce this *Living with Serious Mental Illness* series, there was no doubt in anyone's mind that this should be the first book. There was no doubt that we should start with the difficulties that many new sufferers experience 'getting into the system' and staying there. Around half of the members of the LEAP group have experienced considerable delays in obtaining help for their own or a relative's serious mental illness, and two actually waited ten years between them for a diagnosis, let alone effective help! None of them will forget the misery of trying to cope – in ignorance – with an untreated psychosis over an extended period.

Even more important, members' experience of living with and, in some cases, working with, serious mental illness, has taught them that psychosis is no different to any other disease; that is, the earlier it is treated the better.

2   For a detailed discussion on this subject, see Howe, G. (1991) *The Reality of Schizophrenia*. London: Faber & Faber, pp.77–123.

Getting into the system and staying there

Members of the LEAP group are concerned that they still come across frequent examples of extended delays in 'getting into the system' and in obtaining explanations about serious mental illness and how to survive it. They decided that a careful study of examples of such cases might provide an opportunity to identify any common features which seem to militate against a satisfactory response to a first episode of a serious mental illness. Accordingly, they have made a point of highlighting those factors which seem to influence whether or not a new sufferer will get prompt and effective help. Perhaps equally important, the group has also focused on the sort of factors which may contribute to the sufferer later slipping through the net.

Another way forward?

In some instances, the LEAP group has gone further than this and members have made recommendations which they feel could help to ensure that more sufferers not only obtain effective help promptly but that they also stay safely in the system. Some readers may be heartened by the fact that these recommendations seem to be concerned less with increases in resources than with the setting of a few mandatory baselines which could lead to a more co-ordinated and structured approach to handling serious mental illness. In fact, rather than placing an extra burden on admittedly scarce resources, these recommendations would clearly be cost effective.

CHAPTER 2

Having a diagnosis and not being told

It would seem reasonable to suppose that most of us want to be told what is the matter with us if we are not well, particularly if knowing the truth gives us a better chance of protecting ourselves from any further damage from our illness. Similarly, those close to us usually want to know what they can do to help us if we need this. Let's consider for a moment what happened to Jackie when she and her family were deprived of explanations and information about her serious mental illness.

CASE STUDY

This reserved but warm young woman married the father of her unborn infant when she was four months pregnant and just twenty years of age. She had been very much alone in the world during the previous few years, since her father had married again shortly after her mother's death. His new wife had made it clear that she did not want a teenager around the house and certainly not one who so resembled her dead mother. Estranged from her own family, Jackie was delighted to find Pete's large family so close and welcoming.

Two years after the birth of their first child, a second daughter was born to Jackie and Pete and for a while the couple were very happy. However, several months after this birth, Jackie was finding it increasingly difficult to cope with two infants, always feeling tired and behind with her chores. Pete's work as a salesman kept him away from home some nights and at those times she felt much worse and begun to feel insecure when she was alone in the house.

As time went on, sometimes she would hear 'whispering' on the stairs, but there was never anyone there. At the same time, she begun to suspect that Pete chose to be away from home and that he was seeing another woman. She said nothing to him about any of this but she became snappy with him and kept complaining about her in-laws, telling him they were two-faced and talked about her behind her back.

Pete did what he could to put his wife's mind at rest about her fears about his family for he knew they adored her, and to reassure her that she was a great wife and mother. However, nothing he said or did seemed to help and he eventually persuaded Jackie to go and see their GP.

The doctor was sympathetic and talked with the young woman about the stresses of looking after two young children, particularly with her husband having to be away quite frequently and she eventually admitted to crying a lot and feeling tired and unable to cope most of the time. The doctor prescribed anti-depressants and told Jackie to come back and see him in a month's time.

One evening a week or so later, Jackie suddenly became agitated and hysterical, hurling abuse at her horrified husband, making wild accusations about his 'other woman'. She rushed into the street in her night clothes, screaming at the neighbours, crying that she knew they broke into her house at night when her husband wasn't there, scaring her with their whispering. Chasing after her, Pete called out to his friend next door to call the doctor out and eventually managed to calm Jackie down enough to bring her back indoors. Later that night, the GP persuaded her to go into hospital, telling her she needed a rest from all of her responsibilities and, he suspected, a different type of medication to give her some piece of mind and a chance to feel her old self again.

Four weeks later, Jackie was discharged from hospital, clearly having benefited from the rest and treatment she had been given. The psychiatrist told Pete that his wife had been a little depressed and that this was not unusual in the months after childbirth; he had prescribed new medication for her since she came into hospital and he would like her to stay on this for a while and to come and see him regularly at his out-patient's clinic.

Feeling happier and more confident than she had for a long time, Jackie was happy to go along to her first out-patient appointment and was delighted that the psychiatrist was very pleased with her. However, when she asked about coming off the medication, he said it was too soon to think about this. The same thing happened at her next two out-patient appointments, despite the fact that she felt sure she was now completely well again. She begun to feel restless about persevering with the medication, particularly as Pete's family were anxious about her being on 'those dangerous psychiatric drugs'.

Jackie was really disappointed when she saw a different, young, doctor at her next appointment. She came away with old, familiar, feelings of rejection because the psychiatrist who had seemed so interested in her had now passed her over to someone else. The new doctor had said, 'see you in a month's time, then', and, she gathered, the message was 'keep on taking the medication'.

Jackie talked with Pete, who agreed that his wife was her old self again now. He understood why she didn't want to bother with the out-patient appointments with the new doctor and he was rather relieved as this would mean that she would stop taking this medication she had been on for four or five months now. Pete didn't feel so strongly about it as his parents and sisters did, but he was worried that his wife might become dependent upon these drugs; he'd seen several patients in the hospital who looked like robots and he guessed that this was due to the drugs they were given.

About three months later, Pete started to suspect that Jackie was gradually slipping back to how she'd been before she went into hospital; she was tired and weepy a lot of the time. Before long, she was complaining again that his two-faced parents were poking their noses into her affairs. This confirmed his suspicions that Jackie was not so well after all and when she referred to the 'whispering' on the stairs, he insisted she should go with him and see the GP. Even as he finished saying this, his wife sprung at him, clutching his throat, shouting that he just wanted to put her away again so that he could go to his other woman. He was taken by surprise, amazed at her strength, and only able to restrain Jackie by striking her and gripping her in a vice-like hold. At this point the anger subsided and she sobbed quietly while Pete phoned the doctor. Later that night, she was admitted to hospital.

Once again, Jackie recovered within a few weeks. This time, one of the hospital team who had visited Pete at home and met with the rest of the family, pointed out to the psychiatrist that Jackie and her husband needed to be told what was wrong with her; they needed to be told that she had an acute schizophrenic illness. It seemed very likely, otherwise, that she might be persuaded to come off her medication again. The doctor was not impressed with this argument and said that schizophrenia was a devastating label and he had no intention of burdening the young woman with this. He wanted her to be able to 'just get on with her life' like everyone else. And that was that.

When Jackie was discharged, she and Pete were told that she had suffered a mild repeat of her previous depression, but she should be fine now; the doctor would keep an eye on her at the out-patient's clinic. They both willingly settled for this as Jackie was so obviously her old self again.

After six months had passed, Pete and his parents agreed with Jackie that her medication seemed to be making her sleepy and that this made coping with the children really hard work for her. In fact, she sometimes longed to have a rest for a couple of hours during the day but was too ashamed to mention this, knowing that she must be very inadequate to need a rest at her age. Much to her concern, the medication was apparently causing her to put on weight too; perhaps that explained some of her tiredness? She was obviously so very well otherwise that Pete and the rest of the family enthusiastically supported Jackie when she decided to come off the medication.

It was not long before Jackie's health started to deteriorate again. This time, she needed a longer time in hospital and did not recover in the way she had after her first two breakdowns. Very gradually, the family realized that Jackie had lost her original sparkle and interest in life; she seemed to be apathetic and depressed all the time. By the time she went into hospital for a fourth time, Pete's parents were, to all intents and purposes, looking after the children most of the time and their son was beginning to lose hope for his marriage. Jackie had been moved to a different ward and was now under a new doctor. Pete took the little girls to see her regularly but was often rewarded by very little response. About this time, he was told that his wife was showing all the signs of a chronic schizophrenic illness and that this explained her lack of energy, her lack of interest in herself and others, and her stunted conversation. When he asked why his wife was neglecting her appearance and personal hygiene when she had always been fastidious about such matters, he was told this was all part of the illness too. What Pete didn't understand was how this had happened to her; how the girl he had fallen in love with could have changed so much.

COMMENT

The sort of attitude displayed by the psychiatrist in this case was possibly commonplace in the treatment of cancer fifty years ago. The truth was regularly withheld from patients and this did nothing at all to lessen the stigma and fear associated with this group of diseases. In retrospect, it might be that there was some excuse for professional reticence with cancer in the days when it was often an inevitable killer, but it is hard to find any justification for a similar reticence when the diagnosis is a psychotic illness. In fact, the opposite is true, because this type of illness is treatable and because sufferers are far more likely to avoid further relapse if they are aware of their vulnerability. Equally important, because the majority of cases of schizophrenia – the most common type of psychosis – are first diagnosed in young people in their teens or earlier twenties (1), then ignorance of their condition can lead to much of a potentially long life being wasted.

Perhaps it might be worthwhile to pause for a moment before going on to look at the group's analysis of this case, to make a note of any positive reasons you can think of which justify the withholding of information about their diagnosis from schizophrenia sufferers and their families, and then to consider each of these in the light of my comments and Jackie's experience as revealed in this case study.

GROUP'S ANALYSIS OF CASE STUDY

There was a strong feeling within the LEAP group that Jackie's illness need never have deteriorated into the chronic form of schizophrenia if she had persevered with her medication, probably staying on it indefinitely. Because her GP responded promptly to her dilemma, she was quickly into hospital and receiving the appropriate treatment even while the diagnosis would still have to be a provisional one. The group felt that everything was going right for Jackie at this point and that it was all thrown away because the psychiatrist kept vital information from her and Pete. Why, they asked, did he ignore his colleague's plea to share the diagnosis with his patient and and her husband? How could he expect her to 'just get on with her life' when she was so vulnerable and left in ignorance of what was happening to her?

The problems with stigma

There was a general feeling that Jackie's sad story was all about avoiding the labelling of a young woman with a serious mental illness, and in particular a schizophrenic illness. However, one carer pointed out that this made no sense to him as she had already been 'labelled' with a diagnosis of depression, adding, with feeling, 'ask anyone who has been there!' He was puzzled that the psychiatrist seemed to be content to perpetuate the stigma surrounding schizophrenia by demonstrating that it was OK to have depression, but not schizophrenia. Others were surprised about this too. However, a member of the group who has had to cope with a schizophrenic illness for some years felt this was a common phenomenon. She emphatically agreed with the sentiment about perpetuating the stigma surrounding this illness and she asked, 'just what impression do doctors like this think they are giving their patients when they won't even mention their diagnosis?' She felt that everyone has a right to their diagnosis and that *accepting it* and coming to terms with it is half the battle with schizophrenia. She pointed out that this is very much less likely to be achieved if the patient's doctor is clearly unable to accept it!

Fears of labelling?

Members of the group discussed the popular theory that doctors do not like to label their patients by acknowledging to them that they have a serious mental illness. However, they felt that little credence could be given to this argument because patients and those close to them would be the last people to rush off and broadcast the news to other people, wouldn't they?

A carer felt that giving patients information which by right belonged to them could hardly be termed 'labelling'. The real labelling, she pointed out, took place in the patient's medical notes where doctors write down the name of the illness and are obliged to reveal the diagnosis if they receive requests for this, for example for the purposes of insurance, employment, driving licences, and in certain other circumstances. She had no doubt, therefore, that 'fears of labelling' were really all about finding an excuse to avoid discussing a difficult subject, rather than protecting the patient.

At this point, there were protests from several of the group who had not realized that the information on patients' medical notes were accessible in this way. How could patients be deprived of information which could then be made available to other parties, they wanted to know? How indeed? Although the psychiatrist in this case claimed that he wanted Jackie 'just to get on with her life', even if she had been well enough to do this she could, in fact, have been stopped from doing all sorts of things she might like to do because of information on her file. Worse, she wouldn't even know the reason why.

As one group member who has suffered with manic depression (MD) pointed out, if Jackie and her husband had been told the diagnosis, even when it was still provisional, then she would have been able to make an informed choice to 'come out' and share the information with others if, and when, she wanted to. In her own case, this member had eventually chosen to 'come out' and had soon discovered that she could help others struggling to come to terms with their illness. She now realizes that recovering from a serious mental illness can become a positive focal point in your life, and one which can benefit others too. She believed it was certainly her right to have been allowed to make this choice for herself.

The perils of not being aware of your label

A second survivor emphatically agreed with this viewpoint and added that this was not the only benefit to be had by knowing and understanding your diagnosis. There were others too, such as treatment, support, insight and being able to protect oneself, and none of these were guaranteed *if you were not aware of your label*.

There was little doubt in everyone's minds at this point that this was absolutely true and that the issue here was all about *not being made aware of your own label* rather than 'not being labelled' and, that it might be very helpful to try to persuade those professionals who show reluctance about sharing a diagnosis to understand that this is what matters to the patient.

A need for explanations

There was unanimous agreement within the group that it was essential for Jackie and others to learn as much as possible about their illness. She was paranoid about her husband and her parents-in-law, probably because these were the adults who were most important to her. Both she and they needed to know that it was paranoia causing the problems and not their relationships. As one carer pointed out, 'the word schizophrenia can be devastating but at least Jackie would have understood the weird things which were happening to her; this illness is so frightening it needs to be explained to the sufferer'.

Members noted that not only was her illness frightening, Jackie also suffered with tiredness and feelings of inadequacy. It seemed such a shame, they felt, that she and those around her did not have an opportunity to realize that, far from being inadequate as she feared, Jackie was probably doing very well and that she certainly did need extra help and rest. This would have meant a lot to a young woman who was used to being rejected and who desperately needed to feel that she was valued. A survivor pointed out that 'with the correct diagnosis, the family could learn about the illness and so be able to help Jackie in other ways too', adding that in time, 'the sufferer and family can learn they are not alone and take strength from others who have been there too.'

The role of medication

Another survivor agreed with this comment about the family and pointed out that if they had known the truth, they could have made Jackie feel good about taking her medication. This member felt that Jackie and her husband should have been told that she might need to take the medication permanently and that the analogy with a condition like diabetes, often quoted nowadays (2), would have helped them understand and accept this.

Another member who 'has been there' agreed and added 'things would have been different if Jackie had known the medication was keeping her well; no-one enjoys being ill, you know!'. This survivor also felt that it was ridiculous to expect someone to persevere with medication if they don't know what it is for and that it is irresponsible of doctors if they do not explain the potential benefits and risks of taking these drugs. Other members agreed that this was a very important point, particularly as 'compliance over taking medication' is notoriously poor with this illness. (3)

THE WIDER PERSPECTIVE

By the end of this analysis, the group felt sure that Jackie's tragedy had been preventable. They were concerned that this could, and did, happen to other sufferers too and wondered what could be done about the reluctance of some doctors to share a diagnosis of serious mental illness with their patients and their families.

A withheld diagnosis

One member of the group described what had happened to him and his wife when she first became ill. He was desperately worried that she might never be her old self again and 'despite my asking every day when I visited her in hospital how she was and how she would be in the future, nobody told me anything. With my wife's agreement, I eventually called in another consultant privately for a second opinion and was staggered when he said that he agreed with the diagnosis. I asked him *what* diagnosis? He quickly and briefly explained the important factors about manic depression, and about its treatment and prognosis. This helped me enormously; prior to that I had imagined my wife's condition was irreversible'.

This carer appreciates that the manner in which this sort of information is given 'needs very careful handling' and, perhaps not surprisingly, he suspects that most psychiatrists have no training in this aspect of care.

Another member agreed that this could be the reason for some doctors' reticence, but felt that in her own case any attempt, however modest, at naming her illness and sharing information with her would have met her own need to be treated 'as an intelligent person'. A fellow survivor agreed, saying that in her own case she could then have followed up with questions when she was ready for this. At the very least, she would have had 'a handle, a prognosis, and hope, instead of feelings of despair.

Endorsement by the law

There was complete agreement among the group that patients should have a legal right to know their diagnosis and, particularly so, as doctors cannot withhold that same diagnosis from other parties under certain circumstances.

There was less conviction about the situation when the diagnosis might be provisional only, but even at that stage members felt that the truth about the *implications* of such a diagnosis should be shared. As one carer put it, 'When Jackie was first ill, I think I would have wanted to have been told, in a sensitive fashion, that there was a possibility that the diagnosis was schizophrenia – and what that meant – so that I could take in the news gradually and "catch myself if falling".'

Another member, a survivor herself, said she had no doubt that it should be a 'civil right' to be told your diagnosis, and particularly, as others had already suggested, the *implications* of the diagnosis. She agreed that the way the information was shared could be a sensitive issue, adding 'I feel this should be dealt with by the whole multi-disciplinary team rather than just the doctor, who may not always be the ideal person'. This made good sense to others in the group and a carer added that, in her opinion, whoever first shared information with sufferer and family, the team also had a duty to put them in touch with the relevant voluntary organizations, such as the Manic Depression and National Schizophrenia fellowships and SANE. 'After all', she pointed out, 'they're the ones who specialize in serious mental illness and collect all the available and up-to-date information on psychotic illness' (4). Everyone agreed with this point of view and someone added that they not only provide information and run help-lines, but they also introduce sufferers and their families to others having to live with a serious mental illness. There was a general consensus at this point that, at best, contact with one of these organizations can be a turning point in finding ways to cope and it was better that this should come sooner rather than later.

Perhaps the comment of another member, a carer, summed up the general feeling of the group quite simply with: 'Everyone has the right to full information about health issues, especially when they can affect the rest of your life.' This, everyone agreed, surely applied to Jackie.

SUMMING UP

In this chapter, we have looked at what can happen if sufferers and their families are left in ignorance of a diagnosis of serious mental illness.

The group was particularly saddened by Jackie's story, given that she had responded so well to medication on two occasions. They could not understand why, at a time when so much emphasis in psychiatry is placed on civil rights, there has been no attempt to endorse legally patients' right to know their diagnosis, together with any implications that can help them protect themselves from further damage. It was clear that group members could make a very good case for this seemingly worthy reform.

INFORMATION

The following pieces of information are relevant to points brought up during the author's comment and the group's analysis and discussion which have been highlighted in the text:

(1)   Age-group most likely to develop schizophrenia

One in every one hundred of us will develop a schizophrenic illness at some time in our lives but most sufferers – *80 per cent* – are eventually first diagnosed between 16 and 25 years of age.

(2)   Comparison with diabetes

Back in the 1970s, a leading psychiatrist in the USA pointed out that 'Diabetes mellitus is analogous to schizophrenia in many ways. Both are symptom clusters or syndromes... Each may have many aetiologies and shows a range of intensity from severe and debilitating to latent or borderline. There is also evidence that genetic and environmental influences operate in the development of both.' ('From rationalization to reason', *American Journal of Psychiatry*, September 1974, p.962)

Increasingly psychiatrists in this country point out similarities in the two conditions, also emphasizing that many schizophrenia sufferers have to accept a need to take neuroleptic medication indefinitely for their chemical imbalance in the same way that many diabetes sufferers have to accept a need to take Insulin every day.

(3)   The role of medication

Research findings consistently confirm the medical profession's problems with obtaining compliance from their seriously mentally ill patients in persevering with their medication. However, sufferers and those closest to them continue to report that no-one explains (a) what the medication is for (b) how it has an important role in reducing the risk of relapse as well as in arresting a psychotic breakdown and (c) about the side effects and long-term risks associated with these drugs.

In other words, they are not helped to understand the important role of medication in the treatment of serious mental illness nor enabled to weigh up for themselves the advantages and disadvantages of persevering with taking this.

(4)   Introducing sufferers and carers to organizations specializing in serious mental illness

Sufferers repeatedly report that they only started to cope with what had happened to them when they learned all about their illness and met others 'who have been there too'. Many only achieve this when they make contact with one or other of the voluntary organizations concerned with serious mental illness (see under

Useful Addresses at end of the book). These organizations not only provide opportunities to meet with other sufferers and carers, they provide help–lines, collate up–to–date information and recommend 'tried and tested' literature on their specialist subjects. Busy and pressurized professionals can lighten their workload and help their clients and patients by making these invaluable resources available to them sooner rather than later.

EXERCISE

With schizophrenia, each relapse brings with it the risk of further deterioration or, worse, the onset of the chronic form of the illness and this has been demonstrated in Jackie's case.

In what ways do you feel that potential sufferers' interests can be protected once their symptoms respond to anti–psychotic medication, although it may not be possible to confirm a diagnosis of schizophrenia at that stage?

CHAPTER 3

The pain of not knowing what is wrong

In the last chapter, we looked at what can happen when sufferers and their families are given neither a diagnosis nor any information about the likelihood and dangers of further breakdowns. The following case study reveals more clearly what it *feels* like to know that something is dreadfully wrong without being given any satisfactory explanations for this.

CASE STUDY

A bright and sunny tempered sixteen-year-old, Marie had been feeling 'out of sorts' and inexplicably ill at ease for a couple of days. On top of this, she found that her family – her mother and elder sister – were suddenly being difficult and demanding, even critical. They had seemed surprised when she challenged them about this, saying she must be imagining things. She had ended up in tears. She felt it was not fair of them to 'get at her' when she wasn't feeling herself.

When she went into work the morning after this upset, Marie was aware that everything suddenly went quiet as she walked into the crowded office. So she was right, something was the matter! Even as she glared at those nearest to her, she realized they were watching her in hostile silence. It was as though she was being engulfed by a nightmare in which everyone loathed her and wanted to get rid of her. Someone at a neighbouring desk asked her quietly if she had got out of bed the wrong side this morning? Marie ignored her; she was near to tears. She didn't speak during the next one and a half hours and sat in the office when everyone else went down to the canteen for their 'elevenses' in the middle of the morning. When they returned, several of her colleagues looked curiously at her and asked if she was not feeling well? One, in particular, muttered, 'Oh, leave her to it!', whereupon Marie erupted and turned on her with 'leave me to what?' The woman backed off and Marie swung round on the others, screaming 'do you think I don't know what's going on?' Everyone watched in amazement, as she picked up her computer and, with what seemed to be super-human strength, threw the machine on the floor. Her startled boss rushed across the room, asking what on earth was the matter? Marie burst into tears and sobbed 'you know what's the matter!' Baffled and concerned, he suggested that the young woman take some time off and rest. A friend who worked in the next office came in at the moment to find out why Marie hadn't come down to the canteen and, hearing what had happened, she offered to go home with her and this was agreed.

During the journey, the girls sat in silence. Jane kept a wary eye on her friend, not knowing what to expect next. She carefully sat herself between Marie and the train carriage door. After what seemed like a lifetime, they at last turned into the road where Marie lived, only to find two men fixing the phones outside her house. Of course, Marie realized in horror, they're spies! She saw the way they looked at Jane, smiling and nodding. 'Yes', she exclaimed accusingly' to her friend, 'you're in this, too, aren't you?' and rushed into the house in tears, only to find someone on the telly was talking about her. She didn't stop to hear more; she ran to the set, screaming, trying to smash the screen. When Marie's mother and sister intervened, she rushed upstairs, crying, and only came down again when she realized that the men 'fixing the phones' – clearly stationed there to keep an eye on her – could see into her bedroom. When she walked into the lounge, a commentator was still talking about her on the television and this time she tore the set off its stand. She was fighting on the floor with her sister, who had tried to restrain her, when the family's GP turned up in response to their mother's earlier call for help.

Marie grudgingly agreed to the doctor's suggestion that she should go into hospital. Indeed she felt so ill that she knew she must have a really severe case of 'flu' or worse. However, when the car drew up at the old mental hospital which she and her friends sometimes joked about, Marie begun striking out at everyone, distressed and terrified. She was quickly given an injection to sedate her but it was some hours before she calmed down.

She was very ill during her first weeks in hospital, usually withdrawn and silent but sometimes aggressive, even violent. Much of the nightmare is a blank but she still remembers feeling completely alone and terrified. After several months, however, she was well enough to go home and arrangements were made for her to attend a day-centre. At this point, all she knew was that she had been very ill. It seemed that she was now recovering from some sort of breakdown and was to continue to have injections for a while to help her with this. When she checked this out with her mother, she found that she had no more information than this, so Marie assumed 'that was that', fervently hoping this was the end of her nightmare.

Six weeks later, when she felt she was beginning to find some confidence in herself again, Marie was told by a doctor that she was ready to return to work. She remembers asking a nurse who had been involved in her care in the hospital, to help her. In tears, she explained that she was terrified of going back to the office; she couldn't go back yet, but the nurse told her, 'don't worry, you'll cope!'

For a long while, Marie didn't cope. The office was full of dire memories and she frequently found herself experiencing the same sort of feelings that she had done on that dreadful morning. Feeling quite desperate, she would sometimes phone the hospital and beg to return there. Whenever this happened, she would be told to come in and talk with a nurse. This would calm her down and reassure her a little but then she had to make her way home and it all started again. She says now of the paranoia, 'travelling home on the bus, or just walking down the street was unbearable; everyone was talking about me'. On reaching home, the memories all flooded back; memories of the 'telephone men', of the people on the television talking about her, and of her feelings about her family when all this was happening. Confused and despairing, she tried in vain to sort out what was real and what wasn't real. 'It was a nightmare,' she comments now, 'I needed to be in hospital; I needed some peace'.

When Marie was recovering from her breakdown, she had told doctors about what had happened to her at work and they had explained that she had been ill and her imagination had played tricks on her. Her attempts to get help from nurses in the months after her discharge were based on the hope that someone would at last realize that these dreadful things were in fact happening; she was not imagining them. Instead they kept telling her that she must get on with her life and forget all about these feelings and that the injections would help her to do this. Most of the time, Marie persevered with these, believing them to be some sort of pick-me-up, but what she really craved was the the peace of the hospital; the only place she had eventually been able to escape the torment. She became certain that she must be quite mad, and realized that no-one understood, even the doctors, because she was the only person in the world like this.

This continued for over two years and each time she decided to give up on the injections, or the dose was reduced, Marie ended up in hospital again. 'My diagnosis was a joke', she says now, 'no-one wanted to tell me what was the matter and I couldn't sort out what was happening on my own'. Along the way she realized that other people she knew who were 'on injections' were schizophrenic, but for some time she didn't make the connection with herself because most of them were clearly handicapped by their illness and this was quite obvious; no-one tried to persuade them otherwise. In her own case, however, it seemed that everyone spent their time trying to reassure her that she was not ill; she was a bright and attractive girl who really should be getting on with her life.

It was only when Marie one day angrily demanded to know if she too had schizophrenia, hoping that this would persuade the professionals how much she needed to be told what was really happening to her, that she learned the truth. Yes, it seemed that the doctors did now feel, albeit reluctantly, that all her experiences must be due to an acute schizophrenic illness. After her initial shocked denial, she remembers a profound sense of relief flooding through her; 'at last I understood my symptoms and in a way it gave me reasoning to the madness'. She marvels now that no-one understood the pain she had been experiencing during 'what should have been the best years of my life!'

From this point Marie was able to find a way forward. She quickly learned to look after herself, with her family's support and her new-found confidence enabled her to ask for help when she felt threatened by a return of her symptoms. She has been particularly fortunate in this in having a psychiatrist who always listens to her and responds immediately when she does seek help.

Marie has also found that other professionals have tended to take an interest in her too and that they have usually supported her in her efforts to remain well. However, there have been a few notable exceptions. On three separate occasions during the four years after she learned her diagnosis, she met nurses who tried to persuade her that the doctors were wrong; no-one so 'bright and together' as you could have schizophrenia, they told her. When she said that she longed to be free of having to take medication, these same professionals were quick to encourage her to come off it; to prove she didn't need to take anti-psychotic medication. Because she so wanted to believe them, Marie was seduced each time by their encouragement and promises of support. And, each time, 'I fell flat on my face', as she puts it. Marie finally realized that 'the professionals who wanted to prove to me that I did not have schizophrenia were the same ones who never stayed around to pick up the pieces when I relapsed after coming off the medication'. The professionals who helped her back to good health were those who brought less welcome news, insisting she really must persevere with the medication if she was to get on with the rest of her life. Marie eventually accepted this and has been rewarded with a normal lifestyle and all the things that she had once come to believe were not for her. Occasionally she frets about having to take medication but she has no intention of ever again putting at risk everything she has achieved.

COMMENT

There are plenty of individuals with an acute schizophrenic illness who are as well as Marie. However, we don't hear of many such success stories when we read the literature or talk about schizophrenia. Perhaps Marie's story gives us some indication of the reason for this? Could it be that everyone is so concerned to deny a potentially devastating illness in apparently fit and attractive young people that they lose sight of the fact that the two can go together?

This seems to be quite possible as most professionals involved with this illness tend, naturally, to work with sufferers who are permanently disabled with chronic schizophrenia or with individuals with an acute schizophrenic illness *at times of relapse* – when they are very ill and suffering with all sorts of bizarre symptoms. In other words, many professionals see only the 'down side' of this illness and this may have resulted in their having a depressingly loaded view of schizophrenia. If so, this is a great pity because at least some of these sufferers will be leading rewarding and successful lives most of the time and many others will have a reasonably normal lifestyle between episodes of their illness.

Because of her experience, Marie is more aware than most sufferers that some professionals are preoccupied with the stigma associated with schizophrenia and are therefore very reluctant to label individuals who don't appear to be disabled by the illness. Happily, she is quite vocal about this matter because she is anxious to persuade professionals that a fear of labelling should not get in the way of helping sufferers to understand what has happened to them. This, she believes, is the only way they can come to terms with their illness and protect themselves from further damage. Before moving on to the group's analysis of this case, you might find it worthwhile to pause for a while to note any arguments which support Marie's point of view and consider whether you find them valid and useful.

GROUP'S ANALYSIS OF CASE STUDY

In the last chapter, group members asked questions about the rights of sufferers to know their own diagnosis and to have information about their illness. When analysing Marie's experience, they were more interested in looking for ways to protect the individual from further damage while acknowledging professional reluctance to 'label' a young person.

What to tell?

Members felt that the lack of a diagnosis in the early days of Marie's illness were almost certainly due to well-meaning hopes of doctors that hers might be a 'one off' episode. This seemed to be justified for, as one member pointed out, Marie was very young at the time and it seemed to be generally accepted that there was a much better chance of a good prognosis with this sort of 'sudden-onset' breakdown. However, this carer still felt the risks for the future were too great to leave sufferers and their families in complete ignorance. She felt that they should be given enough information about psychotic illness to have some understanding of what has happened and to be aware of the possibility that there could be a relapse in the future.

Another member agreed in principle, but warned that sufferers themselves might find words such as psychosis and schizophrenia overwhelming in the early stages of recovery, although they certainly needed enough information 'to be getting on with' at this time. This should include discussing symptoms and how these can cause fear and confusion, and in the case of paranoia, disruption of important relationships. 'This sort of information – together with opportunities for testing what is real and what isn't and learning to recognize any lingering symptoms for what they are – can help you to gain some insight into what has happened' she pointed out. Similarly, she felt that patients should be told what the drugs are for and about possible risks and side effects, for 'why on earth should anyone persevere with taking medication, without being given this sort of information?', she asked. This member has survived a schizophrenic illness and rates herself fortunate that this sort of information was given to her gradually and openly from the start.

The group agreed that this approach would have helped Marie and that in particular she would not have felt so desperate and alone if she had known she had symptoms that others suffer with. This sort of explanation would also have helped her to test reality when frightening memories kept flooding back to torment her.

Someone followed this up by pointing out that if Marie's family had been better informed, then they could have given her more information at the time she sought it when she came out of hospital. There was complete agreement on this, with everyone expressing concern that her mother and sister had apparently been left to get on with whatever was happening to Marie as best they could. This did not help anyone, least of all Marie as she had become paranoid about those closest to her during her illness. Later, when all was revealed, it seemed that the family were able to provide the support Marie needed. Meanwhile, there was a danger that they might have felt previously that she should 'snap out of it', particularly as some of the professionals seemed to be giving Marie this message.

Assessing the seriousness of the illness

There was general agreement within the group that no-one seemed to appreciate the severity of Marie's symptoms and that she was still very vulnerable when she came out of hospital. Members felt that it should have been apparent just how frail she was when it was suggested she was ready to return to work, but a survivor pointed out that Marie may not have revealed this to the doctors; it seemed she chose always to talk to nurses about her problems and they may not have recognized what was happening to her.

Members agreed that Marie, like many before her, may have worked very hard at appearing 'well and together' (and not *mad*, as she put it) with doctors and this may not have served her best interests. Her doctors didn't seem to know how desperately confused Marie was over a very long period and earlier on may have been deceived into thinking she could cope with returning to work much sooner than was the case. A survivor explained 'it's a great pity but this sort of misunderstanding is common – I sometimes used to confide in "more available" professionals when I needed help, in the vain hope that my concerns would be passed on to the "all powerful" doctor!'

Professional help since the diagnosis

Everyone agreed that a very positive feature in this case, and one which has stood her in good stead throughout her recovery, has been the immediate response given to Marie by the psychiatrist whenever she has sought his help. Members felt that not only did this ensure she was protected, but it also provided just the sort of feedback Marie needed to take responsibility for her own wellbeing successfully. This contrasted sharply with her experiences when she was entirely dependent on others for this.

The question of individual professionals openly challenging the diagnosis shocked and dismayed some members. However, one was not surprised and declared 'Oh, no, I've been there too'. She told the group of her own experience of this sort of attitude when recovering from a relapse at a day hospital. The staff had apparently abandoned a 'medical model' of schizophrenia and they kept prodding her to have some confidence in herself and to stop relying on medication to make her well. On one occasion, she had to steel herself at the end of the day to go into the nurses' room because they had not called her in for her injection earlier ('and you have to be mad to beg for an injection, you know!', she laughed). The manager, a senior professional, greeted her with 'Oh, we hoped you would stop this nonsense and prove to us all that you can manage without yet another injection!' She was completely mortified and ran out of the room in tears. 'Well', she told the group, 'I only got my injection when another professional threatened to report any further problems to my psychiatrist – I have often wondered how sufferers with less insight into their illness fared at that place'.

Members of the group were concerned enough at this point to agree that this matter needed further consideration when the group came to discuss 'the wider perspective' of this case study. Everyone agreed that it was a sad indictment on some very questionable practice that the professionals who encouraged Marie to come off her medication were the same ones who never stayed around to give her support when she relapsed. This certainly precluded any ideas that they had her welfare at heart.

Finally, the group as a whole felt cheered by the very positive ending to Marie's story while nevertheless agreeing with one carer's comment that it was 'desperately sad for a young person to have such a terrifying experience alone'.

THE WIDER PERSPECTIVE

Members returned at this point to the subject of withholding the diagnosis in the hope that a schizophrenic breakdown may be a 'first and only' episode.

A popular statistic

Several members of the group were aware of the widely accepted theory that at least 25 per cent of all individuals having a schizophrenic breakdown have no further incidence of the illness (1) and that this is the reason that some psychiatrists give for not wanting to acknowledge a first episode. Regardless of the accuracy or otherwise of this statistic, the feeling in the group was that withholding a diagnosis for this reason was 'not on!' 'How,' someone wanted to know, 'can there be any justification for leaving the vast majority of sufferers in ignorance of what has happened to them and therefore unable to protect themselves?' Because members of the LEAP group are confident that dangerous relapses can be avoided when sufferers and those close to them are well informed, they were appalled by an approach which actually involves waiting for a second breakdown to happen in order to confirm a provisional diagnosis. As a carer pointed out, 'any fears about stigma become redundant if this second breakdown is one too many and the sufferer lapses into the chronic form of the illness'.

Whose hang-ups?

Similarly, members could not understand why there should be so much reluctance to share a diagnosis of schizophrenia or other serious mental illness once this has been determined. One carer pointed out that when Marie obtained information and knowledge about her illness, her quality of life improved dramatically. This did not surprise him because most of the sufferers he comes across in his work in the voluntary sector claim to have coped better once they learned their diagnosis, albeit manic depression or schizophrenia. He wondered why so many professionals seem to be unaware of this important fact? Other members agreed that this is the message they receive too and they wondered how they could get this point across to mental health professionals? There was a general feeling in the group that some professionals have more hang-ups about a diagnosis of serious mental illness (particularly when it might be schizophrenia) than those who have to get on with coping with the condition. This, they were sure, did nothing at all to lessen the stigma associated with it. All agreed that Marie was right to feel so deeply about wanting to change professional attitudes on this.

The challenging of a diagnosis

Members returned to the vexing question of some professionals being prepared to challenge a diagnosis once this has been established and several asked how this could come about? This led to discussion about the growing rivalry over recent years between the health professions which led to each favouring different theories of mental illness. Several of the group, who have worked with, or within, one of the caring professions offered the following comments in answer to queries from other members:

'Yes; there's this rivalry between the professions which leads to emphasis on theories which don't allow for illness as such. For example, social work training seems to be preoccupied with seeing mental illness as a way to scapegoat and label people (2) – so you can put them away, I suppose! And then social workers look for causes other than illness for what is going wrong – and you can always find them if you want to, you know!'

'Yes, and the nursing profession has tended to move away from doctors and their 'medical model' as well and emphasize 'behavioural' or 'social' problems in their patients (3).'

'That's right, and they don't really learn about schizophrenia as an entity now, do they? So they're less likely to recognize the illness or understand how it affects the way someone behaves. They claim they treat 'the presenting behaviour' – but, how can you do that if you don't understand what's causing the behaviour?'

'Well, I've noticed that where patients are obviously 'mad', then nurses are very considerate and sympathetic and seem to take it as read that they have an illness. However, they don't seem to realize that some individuals can be mad enough to keep quiet about their psychotic ideas and to control their behaviour – I know this from my own experience!'

'Yes, I believe that the nurses who later challenged the diagnosis and encouraged Marie – and our colleague too! – to come off their medication just don't recognize psychosis in someone who is not obviously bizarre and disabled. It's a pity – nurses used to know more about this type of illness years ago.'

These comments led to a general discussion on the various theories and attitudes prevalent in the caring professions today and to a conviction that more progress might be made if everyone 'pulled together' and pooled their knowledge and expertise. 'And', someone concluded, 'they could start by listening more to Marie and others who have been there.

SUMMING UP

In this chapter the group looked at the predicament of an intelligent young woman trying to cope with a serious mental illness which was, to all intents and purposes, denied. Members felt it was a great pity that Marie had to wait so long for the information she needed. They applauded her efforts to persuade professionals that they shouldn't be so pre-occupied with stigma and fears of labelling; these, they knew, were not the main concerns of sufferers themselves.

LEAP group was perturbed to learn that when Marie was making real progress, several professionals could voice their opinions that her hard-won diagnosis was wrong and, worse, encourage her to come off the medication. This highlighted the very different viewpoints and approaches of the various professions involved in working with serious mental illness and some of the obstacles this can present for sufferers and their families. Members felt that these variations in beliefs and approaches could only detract professionals from pooling their resources and building up a worthwhile body of knowledge about psychosis and psychotic behaviour. Finally, they wondered if this explained why so many mental health professionals chose to avoid working with serious mental illness?

INFORMATION

The following pieces of information are relevant to points raised during the group's analysis and discussion which have been highlighted in the text:

(1)   A questionable 'statistic'?

Bleuler's finding that 'at least 25 per cent of all schizophrenics recover entirely (after one breakdown) and remain recovered for good' have been widely accepted and quoted. (Bleuler, M. (1978) 'The long-term course of schizophrenic psychoses.' In Wynne, Cromwell and Matthysse (eds) *The Nature of Schizophrenia*. New York: Wiley, pp.631–6.)

This finding is frequently used as justification for avoiding a diagnosis of schizophrenia, and the stigma which goes with it, unless and until such time as a first-time sufferer has a further breakdown. This sort of reasoning appears to leave no less than 75 per cent of sufferers – whose illness can be expected to persist – unprotected and in ignorance of their potential vulnerability to relapse until such time as this in fact happens!

An interesting aspect of Bleuler's finding is less well known, ie, his criteria for 'recovery' apparently allow for the *persistence of delusions and perceptual disturbance*. Bearing in mind the distress such symptoms can cause, even when the sufferer has insight into them, it would seem that the 25 per cent of sufferers who avoid further breakdown might also benefit from a diagnosis, explanations and ongoing support.

(2)   An aspect of social work training

Social work training has been influenced for decades by the theories of individuals such as the late R.D. Laing, British psychiatrist, despite the fact that he himself seemed to have difficulty identifying, let alone understanding, them himself. He is reporting as saying in 1982:

'I don't think I could pass an exam question on what is R.D. Laing's theory. I was looked to as one who had the answers but I never had them' ('Britain's Offbeat Psychiatrist', *Newsweek*, 1 November 1982, p.16, quoted in E. Fuller Torrey (1988) *Surviving Schizophrenia*, revised edition (New York: Harper and Row).

Laing's writings debunked psychiatry and pronounced schizo-phrenia to be an appropriate response to unacceptable pressures from society and from families in particular. While accusing fami-lies of scapegoating their sick relative, this school of thought had no hesitation in scapegoating those closest to the sufferer and blaming them for what had happened. Thus, the sort of conflict that ASWs find when they visit homes at the time of a psychotic crisis tends to reinforce ideas learned at college about disfunc-tional families.

Interestingly, a survey of social workers who had completed their ASW training involving 70 days of specialization in mental health legislation and mental illness, revealed that they did not feel they knew enough about the mentally ill and matters con-cerning the mentally ill. (CCETSW paper No 19.25, 'Refresher Training for Approved Social Workers', February 1990.)

(3)   An aspect of psychiatric nursing training

For example, the nurses' English and Welsh National Boards Training Syllabus of 1982 highlighted the need for *a change from a medical model to a social model*. Similarly, a much recommended book, G. Dexter's and M. Wash (1986) *Psychiatric Nursing Skills – a Patient-Centred Approach* (London: Croom Helm), introduced as 'a core text for psychiatric nurses in training' makes two fleeting ref-erences to schizophrenia in its 370 pages, while, for example, de-voting a whole chapter to 'Human Sexuality'.

EXERCISE

In the mental health services, individual professional bodies use markedly different approaches to the handling of conditions such as MD and schizophrenia. These different approaches are based on conflicting theories of psychosis. LEAP group have queried if these differences affect the basic knowledge base available to those working with serious mental illness. In this respect, it may be relevant that many sufferers and their families do not obtain the explanations and basic information they need until they join one of the voluntary organizations specializing in this type of illness.

Do you think that the conflict of approaches and theories regarding the handling of psychosis may affect the basic knowledge base available to those working with this type of illness and do you think this conflict may prejudice opportunities for individual professionals who may wish to specialize in this area?

CHAPTER 4

Teetering on the edge of the system

Sometimes families seek help for a relative who is clearly becoming very ill and obtain a positive response from professionals, only to find later that the sufferer is not really 'in the system' at all. The following case study reveals what happened to one such family.

CASE STUDY

When Barry was 17 years of age, his parents became worried about him. Always something of a loner, this had become more pronounced when the family moved to a new town a couple of years previously. Nevertheless, Barry had been doing well on a foundation course at the local college when he suddenly started to find excuses for not attending the lectures and instead spent much of his time in his bedroom. The room itself was looking stranger all the time; it was cluttered with newspapers and with all sorts of paraphernalia stacked up all over the floor in frenzied piles, sometimes almost to ceiling level. His parents were puzzled about this as Barry had been obsessionally tidy throughout his childhood but now made no attempt to tidy or clean up and refused to let his mother into the room when she offered to do this for him. In fact, he had gradually distanced himself from his parents and no longer joined them for meals or took up his usual niche in the living-room to watch the early evening 'soaps'. He rarely went out during the day but would go off walking for hours at night. Apart from this he did nothing and saw no-one.

When the family had moved from London, Barry's mother had become depressed and she now contacted the community nurse (CPN) who had helped her through that phase in her life. When the CPN visited the home she was worried enough about Barry to come back later with a colleague who agreed the young man's behaviour was bizarre and seemingly psychotic. A domiciliary visit was arranged via the GP and the psychiatrist decided this was 'real madness', as she put it. She prescribed medication and asked the CPN to keep in touch with the family while she arranged admission to a local day hospital. This took some considerable time, involving a long wait before the CPN was asked to bring Barry along for two separate interviews and then another wait before he could be fitted into the timetable. Meanwhile, Barry's parents knew that he had a mental illness and would need medication and support.

Barry was eventually offered several short sessions a week and the CPN explained to the parents that the doctor at the hospital would look after his medication and treatment. This all seemed quite satisfactory to them and for the first two months he attended there, the CPN liaised with the staff team and kept regularly in touch with the family. At this point, however, she left the area and the parents realized very much later that Barry attended the hospital as little as possible after she left but that prescriptions for his medication were still provided for him as well as appointments to see the psychiatrist supervising his treatment. Barry never told his parents about the appointments, which he stopped attending when the CPN left, nor did he take his medication.

Things went from bad to worse over the next twelve months and eventually the day hospital gave up on Barry when they had not seen him for some time. It took another few months before the parents could get anyone to listen to them again and this time Barry was referred to a local day centre. Very shortly after he started there, staff were reporting to their manager that although the young man seemed to be attending the centre a couple of times a week, he was managing to avoid them and the other clients; in fact it was a case of 'now you see him, now you don't'. They also commented on his poor personal hygiene. The manager eventually found an opportunity to talk with Barry when he came into the centre one morning, limping badly. In answer to the older man's query, Barry shrugged and muttered something about blisters. However, he agreed to let a CPN have a look at these when she visited the centre and she was horrified at the state of his feet which were covered with sores and looked as if they had never seen soap and water. She arranged for these to be seen and dressed at the local Casualty department.

When the nurse reported back to the centre manager, he suggested she should make a home visit to Barry's parents. She found them touchingly grateful to make contact at last with a health professional again and they explained that their home had become a war zone; they had learned to keep out of Barry's way as much as possible because he became hostile and aggressive if they approached him. He kept his room locked and his mother left him to help himself to food from the fridge as he would not sit down and eat a meal with them. Similarly, they had had no success in trying to influence his personal hygiene and they were most concerned about this as Barry had been clean, even fastidious, before things had started to go wrong.

At this point, Barry was referred to the psychiatrist who serviced the centre, and the manager invited the parents to come along for the appointment. The specialist told them that Barry had schizophrenia and that he could only be helped in hospital; she would arrange for him to come in as soon as she could make a bed available for him. A month later, Barry was admitted to hospital under a section allowing for treatment of his mental illness. It was now over two years since the first CPN had sought help for him.

In hospital, Barry was once again prescribed an anti-psychotic drug and this time he had no choice but to take the medication. His parents were delighted to see him making some real progress and also that he was prepared to talk with them a little when they visited.

Six weeks later, the psychiatrist who had admitted Barry and supervised his treatment decided that he was doing very well but that he could benefit from a longer stay in hospital in order to be helped with his damaged social and living skills. He was transferred to a rehabilitation ward and this meant that he came under the supervision of yet another psychiatrist; one that the parents never met. Within a week or so of this move, Barry's medication was reduced. When the parents queried this, the nurse in charge told them that their son did not have schizophrenia or, for that matter, any other illness that required drugs. When Barry's mother protested, pointing out they had waited a long time to see him start to get well again, the nurse shrugged, saying it seemed more likely that his problems were due to poor family relationships. Despite this comment, no attempt was made to meet with the parents to discuss this viewpoint, nor to provide any family sessions. Once more, Barry started to shun his parents and very soon they were told by ward staff that it was not a good idea for them to come to the ward as their visits only upset their son.

Three months later, Barry was discharged to a hostel where he just about coped, avoiding his peers and the staff and regularly going missing at night-time. By now he would have nothing at all to do with his parents. After continued reports from the staff team about his abnormal behaviour, a new doctor eventually raised the dose of Barry's medication to the level being prescribed before he moved to the rehabilitation ward. Very shortly, he started to make some progress again, mixing a little with others in the hostel and discontinuing his midnight prowls around the neighbourhood. He still refused to have anything to do with his parents but staff encouraged them to keep visiting. They found this increasingly difficult as their son seemed quite hostile towards them. His mother begun to despair that they would ever enjoy a good relationship with their son again, but other mothers whom she met when visiting the hostel urged her not to give up.

After a while, the doctor now supervising the young man's treatment decided to raise the dose of his medication further and very quickly everyone noted a dramatic improvement in Barry's mood and lifestyle. He started to make friends with other young people at the hostel, organized several shopping expeditions and trips to the local pub and was friendly and co-operative with staff. Even more significant, he appeared to enjoy his parents' visits and one evening a member of staff telephoned to ask if Barry might pop round and see them? This was the first of his now frequent visits. The family is now reunited and Barry is happily settled at the hostel and planning to return to college to complete his studies. It had taken over three years to rescue this sufferer from 'real madness.'

COMMENT

Group members were deeply concerned about several aspects of this case and when trying to determine, with some difficulty, at which point Barry actually 'got into the system', the question was asked, '*what system?*' The most striking thing for them about the handling – or mishandling – of Barry's illness was a lack of communication between professionals, which was only outmatched by their lack of communication with the parents. For most of the involved professionals, it was as if Barry didn't have a family, despite the fact that the parents were the only individuals providing continuity and a safety net of any kind.

It might be worth while to take a pause and look at this particular aspect of this case before going on to look at the group's analysis. Assume for a moment that you are Barry's mother or father, back at the time when they first sought help for him. What sort of information and support you would be wanting from professionals involved with your son? Similarly, what contribution do you, as one of Barry's parents, feel that you could have offered the professionals if you had been asked?

GROUP'S ANALYSIS OF CASE STUDY

Members were frankly amazed by the lack of any sort of co-ordination and continuity revealed in this case study. A carer pointed out that this could not even be blamed on difficulties sometimes encountered with inter-agency working as it could be assumed that the hospital, day hospital, CPNs and consultants would all work for the same service provider. 'Yet', he pointed out, 'there was no evidence of any sort of systematic review of Barry's case'.

Others marvelled at the lack of communication 'between and from professionals' and in particular singled out the way the family had been ignored as a potential resource and a unit to be nurtured and supported. One carer commented that 'they failed Barry right at the start because they failed to include the parents, so that he and they knew what was involved with this illness all of the time'. The group decided that proper communication between professionals and family was so important that they would return to this subject in their discussion after this analysis. Meanwhile, they focused on highlighting the breaks in communication and continuity revealed in Barry's story.

First CPN

At the start of the case study, the CPN who responded quite informally to a call for help from Barry's mother quickly found herself to be the key worker in this case because the psychiatrist who made the domiciliary visit left it to the nurse to follow up the referral to the day hospital and to arrange Barry's admission. However, shortly after this, the nurse left the district. The group were puzzled and dismayed that when she left – the only professional providing any continuity for Barry and his family, someone noted – the CPN was not replaced. How could this happen? A member, who has herself worked in 'the system', explained that CPNs are usually in short supply and patients who are attending a resource such as a day hospital are presumed to be monitored regularly by its staff team. 'This, of course, is what should have happened this time', she added.

First psychiatrist

Members wanted to know what this doctor meant by 'real madness'? They knew that doctors used to call psychosis 'madness' in the old days and they therefore felt that the doctor was acknowledging a psychotic illness in Barry. They also felt that the word 'real' implied there was very little doubt about this in her mind. Why then, they wanted to know, was there no urgency about starting treatment for Barry and making sure he was stabilized on appropriate medication? Members did not believe it was reasonable to expect this to happen without the sort of daily monitoring which can be carried out in hospital. The day hospital, they noted, did not seem to be geared into responding to urgent need of any sort; their referral system was protracted and cumbersome and the psychiatrist must have been aware of this beforehand.

The group found the doctor's attitude to be, at best, casual and, at worst, uncaring. 'Surely,' said one of the mothers in the group, 'she realized that with his recent history, and something she called "madness", Barry would not have attended the day hospital for long?'

The day hospital

With the CPN gone, it seemed the parents had now lost touch with 'the system' and Barry's contact with it was tenuous, to say the least. He turned up at the day hospital occasionally and the staff team arranged for him to have prescriptions (which he didn't use) and appointments to see a psychiatrist (which he didn't keep).

The group couldn't understand how Barry's non-involvement with the day hospital, once the CPN left, didn't attract attention or concern. A member, who is also a survivor, said that this suggested a lack of *caring* which she found very sad and worrying. Others nodded in agreement with this and with a carer's comment that it also suggested 'a lack of understanding and knowledge about psychotic illness – and this goes for some of the other professionals in this case too'.

Another member felt that 'at the very least, there would seem to be a clear need for a follow-up system for psychiatric patients who fail to attend appointments – anyway, when two outpatient appointments have been missed. There was a general feeling in the group that 'not following up missed appointments is a common failing in the system' and that there seemed to be little or no recognition of the fact that unkept appointments in a serious mental illness have to be a cause for concern.

Finally, most of the the group were at a loss for words when it came to the day hospital 'giving up' on their patient. However, one member explained with a wry smile that the staff team at some of these frequently well-funded resources work on the principle that they only keep patients on their register who themselves acknowledge that they want to attend and who are prepared to co-operate with their treatment. Similarly they are expected to take responsibility for their own medication. 'None of this is likely to be a realistic aim for patients while they are psychotic', she pointed out, 'and perhaps this explains a lack of experience and expertise with the Barrys of this world?'

The first psychiatrist – revisited

This last comment brought the topic back to the psychiatrist and the group's general feeling that referring this young man to the day hospital had not been appropriate – at that time anyway – and what he had needed was to be admitted to a hospital for 24-hour care and stabilizing on his medication.

The day centre

Members were cheered to note there was an effective feedback system at the centre and, more important, that there was evidence of real caring too. The manager quickly followed up the concerns of his staff and also involved a CPN to check out what was happening in the home. The parents were then invited to accompany their son when he saw the new psychiatrist, and this was a first! All agreed with someone's comment that the service provided by the day centre was businesslike and professional.

Admission to hospital

It was not clear what was on the file regarding Barry's diagnosis but, either way, this psychiatrist lost no time in telling the parents the nature of Barry's illness and went on to admit him into hospital when she had one of her own beds to spare. At the point that he left her ward, Barry was making progress and, members felt, there was every reason to believe that he was on the way to making a good recovery (as eventually happened much later).

Transfer to rehabilitation ward

The group was really very concerned about the dramatic lack of continuity in Barry's treatment when he was transferred to another ward. This, they felt, to be unreasonable after all that had gone before. They wanted to know if there was any liaison between the two psychiatrists? No-one could answer this but it seemed unlikely that a bed would have been obtained on the second ward without a proper referral from the first ward and, anyway, Barry's file must have moved on with him. One mother expressed her frustration with 'these doctors who seem so willing to take patients off their medication when they are doing well', as indeed happened with her own son.

A survivor felt that the parents should have asked to speak with the doctor at the point that they were told by a nurse that Barry's diagnosis was wrong. She said that, speaking from her own experience in hospital, 'if the nursing staff do not agree with the diagnosis, you can be told one thing by one person and another by somebody else'. A carer agreed with this and was quite certain that the parents should have checked that the psychiatrist did share the nurse's opinion, and that they should, anyway, have asked the doctor why he had now reduced Barry's medication just as he was starting to do well. While other members felt that this would have been the obvious course to take, they also pointed out that lay people are frequently timid about approaching professionals and they did feel that nothing in these parents' experience would have given them much confidence in that direction!

Finally, the group remained concerned that the rehabilitation ward team did not appear to re-think their hasty decision when Barry's condition deteriorated to the point that he had reached before coming into hospital. Members found it worrying that the supervising doctor and other staff could have been satisfied with this sort of outcome in their patient when the young man had started to make good progress on the first ward.

A new psychiatrist and hostel staff-team

Members noted that the doctor servicing the hostel eventually responded to the staff-team's reports about Barry's inappropriate behaviour and increased his very low dose of medication and later, on the basis of further observation of his progress and behaviour, increased this again. This seemed to the group to be a reassuring example of liaison between those working with Barry on a daily basis and the professional responsible for supervising his treatment. Indeed, a carer pointed out that this was reminiscent of how this type of illness used to be treated – 'find the right medication by starting with a trial dose and gradually increase to the point that the sufferer could be seen to be making real progress!' After a pause, a survivor commented 'this could have been achieved for Barry right at the start, if only someone had got their act together, couldn't it?'

A mixed service

LEAP group were worried about evidence of a lack of basic caring in some of the professionals involved with this vulnerable family. A mother summed up the general feeling within the group with 'Barry's parents seem to have been largely ignored in all of this, being left to struggle on against all the odds – an appalling and very sad story of real suffering for everyone involved.'

On a happier note, everyone agreed that there were also examples of good and caring practice; two of the psychiatrists, both CPNs, the day centre manager and the hostel staff team had provided a caring and effective service. A mother summed up the general feeling with 'it is so good to see how well Barry is doing now – to see yet again that schizophrenia is treatable and sufferers can lead a reasonable life.'

THE WIDER PERSPECTIVE

This last comment left the group asking just how many professionals were really aware that this is the case; just how much opportunity was there for professionals and other workers to learn from a case history such as this one?

A lack of feedback?

Just how much feedback, members asked, do professionals have about the results of their own work with the seriously mentally ill? Would, for example, the staff team on the rehabilitation ward – and some of the other professionals involved in this case – have learned about what happened to Barry after he left the hospital and about his later progress? It seemed to the group that this sort of feedback was essential if the unnecessary suffering revealed in this case study was to be avoided.

Nevertheless, there was a strong feeling within the group that the only sort of feedback that took place was the informal kind where, for example, someone might say to a friend working on the rehabilitation ward, 'have you heard about Barry X; he's doing really well in Y hostel? He's gone back to college and is having a decent social life too', obtaining an answer on the lines of 'I'm not surprised; we knew he'd be OK once he got away from those parents.' Members came up with several similar examples of this kind, all of which allowed faulty ideas and practice to be perpetuated. What was needed, they insisted, was detailed feedback which would give professionals an opportunity to learn what actually does work and what doesn't. Not only would this make it more difficult to adhere rigidly to ideas and theories favoured by individual professional training schemes, it would also provide encouragement for those whose practice really does work. It was felt this was particularly important, for, as one member put it, 'we're talking about people's lives here!'

The group felt there there was a real case for mental health service providers to carry out a brief analysis of what happens in every case of serious mental illness to determine what helps and what hinders a speedy and successful recovery. This would enable agencies to determine what is, and what is not, good practice and would provide a learning tool for the professionals involved in individual cases. Members were quick to point out that this would save 'the system' wasting considerable sums of money as well as improving the services provided.

GPs as key workers?

Some members of the group were amazed at the number of psychiatrists and other professionals involved in Barry's case. Others were less surprised because they have experienced a similar lack of continuity in services themselves. One said she couldn't fault the support her son received from the CPN service but he had had four different nurses in as many years and found it very difficult to cope with each new loss. Another member had lost her psychiatrist of many years when he retired a few years ago. She was admitted to hospital by a new doctor who immediately changed her diagnosis of 30 years' standing! Her medication was also changed accordingly and it took her a couple of years to get really well again and have her previous diagnosis re-established together with the appropriate treatment. The point she wished to make was that it was her GP who eventually sorted out this fiasco for her. She felt that Barry and his family would have been much better served by having a GP involved in their case. This doctor could have provided continuity and 'might have been able to moderate the judgement of the different consultants'. This seemed to be valuable comment and members also felt that a GP could have intervened on the parents' behalf when they didn't even know whom to contact, let alone what questions to ask! The patient's GP could expect to obtain some relevant information.

This brought the group discussion to the feature of this case which worried it most; the treatment of Barry's parents.

The family – the forgotten resource?

Members were concerned that few professionals seem to see relatives as a valuable source of information, let alone the main providers of community care. In Barry's case, some of the professionals involved just ignored the parents or, worse, condemned them out of hand and yet, as one carer pointed out, 'they were the "experts" on Barry's illness – or, rather, its history – and provided the only continuity throughout the time he waited for effective treatment'.

Group members went on to consider what they would have wanted from professionals if they had been Barry's parents and these are some of the answers they came up with:

'Involvement from the start in a proper care plan, pro-active support and the right information. To be treated with some dignity and to be recognized as the major provider of community care for Barry.'

'Information, support, and a hospital admission for my son right at the start. Later, more liaison and explanations, such as why his medication was reduced and discounted when he was doing so well.'

'To be kept up-to-date on his medication and doctor's appointments so that I could have made sure he benefited from these. And to be told why one doctor changed the previous doctor's diagnosis and medication.'

'Someone to talk to, to share concerns with, to get information from. To be involved in checking my son was attending day hospital and what medication he was meant to be taking. To be involved in hospital treatment and in discussion about his change of treatment.'

'To be told all about what was the matter with him and how we could help him, but most of all to be told all about paranoia and why our son was treating us like this – to give us some hope!'

All of these requirements seem to be completely reasonable. Members felt that if this sort of help was offered to the family, then the sufferer would clearly benefit. Again and again throughout the analysis and this discussion, members pointed out that, if they'd been given the chance, the parents could have made sure that Barry took his medication and kept his appointments with doctors. There was a general feeling that, incredibly, 'no-one else was prepared to take the responsibility for this!'

A young survivor summed up everyone's feelings at the close of this discussion with 'I don't understand why families can't be involved with the system; after all they bear the brunt of what happens, along with the individual who has the illness'. Members shared this feeling and, indeed, some had taken part in a survey of a local carers' group several years earlier which confirmed just how much most families are left in the dark about things which matter (1).

SUMMING UP

The group found plenty to alarm them in Barry's story and decided that he and his family had first and foremost been victims of 'the system' rather than victims of a serious illness. It was very clear that when he at last received appropriate treatment and care, and when his parents received some moral support, then all of them were able to get on with their lives. Everyone agreed that this case had lacked co-ordination, continuity and, in several instances, evidence of communication between the professionals concerned, let alone between the professionals and the patient and his family.

Members were concerned that those professionals whose methods of intervention are not helpful rarely seem to obtain any feedback on this and the LEAP group felt that agencies responsible for providing mental health services should arrange for such feedback to be made available. They are confident that a brief analysis of each case would quite quickly start to highlight what works and what doesn't, thus saving avoidable personal suffering and unnecessary public spending.

INFORMATION

The following information is relevant to a point brought up during the group's analysis and discussion which has been highlighted in the text:

(1)   A local carers' group survey

This small, unpublished survey involved 21 out of a possible 22 families and they judged the following nine services to be a priority *at the time of a first episode* of a serious mental illness:

(i)   Support for the family
(ii)   Explanations about the illness
(iii)   Explanations about the way that symptoms may affect the sufferer
(iv)   Explanations about the role of medication and any side effects
(v)   The potential risks of further breakdown
(vi)   A 'lifeline' – what to do if needing help in the future
(vii)   Introduction to self-help organizations and relevant literature
(ix)   Information for *the sufferer* about the illness and how to cope

Over 80 per cent of the families received none of these perceived priorities *at the time of the first episode* of the sufferer's illness. Furthermore, 50 per cent had never received most of them at the time of the survey, despite further opportunities for this at times of relapse. Just one family received most of these services at the start of the sufferer's illness. (Cooper and Howe (1993) reported in Howe, G. (1994) *Working with Schizophrenia*. London: Jessica Kingsley, pp.44–45, further discussion, pp.73–76)

EXERCISE

There is plenty of evidence of families being undervalued by professionals, despite the fact that they are the major providers of community care. Moreover, there is little recognition of their potential role in facilitating a more lasting and successful treatment of their relative's serious mental illness.

Let's imagine that it becomes mandatory for professionals to 'work in partnership' with the close relatives of the sufferers; how would you go about ensuring this is achieved as a matter of course and in what ways do you feel that such a policy could benefit sufferers?

CHAPTER 5

Juvenile sufferers
A special case

Not only does a diagnosis usually bring with it the bonus of appropriate treatment, it can also provide an explanation for nightmarish experience and access to information and to others 'who have been there' themselves. What, then, of those who struggle on indefinitely without any of these benefits and with their problems still unresolved? This can happen wherever there is a reluctance to diagnose and it does seem that this reluctance is never greater than when the sufferer is young; that is, young enough to be referred to the child psychiatry service. Consider for a moment what happened to Malcolm and his family.

CASE STUDY

A sociable and gifted 16–year–old, Malcolm was studying for his 'A' levels, when he suddenly started finding fault with everyone. His family could do nothing right and very soon he was avoiding his close friends and refusing to go to school.

Within a few months, Malcolm was spending the daytime lying on his bed and most of the night prowling around the house. He wouldn't eat with the rest of the family and made dreadful scenes if they sat down to watch television because it was 'too noisy'. He would then go to his bedroom and play a couple of favourite tapes over and over again at full volume. His two small brothers, still at primary school, became nervous and edgy in his company and their father decided matters were getting out of hand and that they needed expert help.

When he approached the family's GP, she was sympathetic and said she would find an excuse to have a close look at Malcolm when this was viable; he tended to come to the surgery quite frequently. She kept her promise and two months later decided that her patient was depressed and she eventually persuaded him to see a psychiatrist. As a result of this, Malcom agreed, with some reluctance, to go into an adolescent psychiatric unit for assessment. He was there for four weeks and was discharged without having received treatment. The psychiatrist and his staff team met once with the parents, with everyone present including Malcolm, and told them that there was nothing to worry about; nothing that was unusual in adolescence. He suggested that they and Malcolm should attend for family therapy sessions with two members of the staff team; a nurse and a social worker.

In the event, Malcolm ran out of the first family therapy session and refused to take any further part in this therapy. No comment was made about this by the therapists and no action was taken. The parents persevered but came away frustrated after each session. When they were given to understand that they were 'too demanding' of Malcolm and also 'under-rating his need for independence at this time', they explained that, on the contrary, they were actually concerned that he was becoming much too dependent upon his mother and refusing to leave the house. When they received no reply to this and similar comments, the parents lost heart and, indeed, after the sixth session the therapists told them there was little point in continuing with the therapy. No offer of further help was forthcoming.

A couple of months later, Malcolm's behaviour was becoming more and more worrying; he would lie on his bed most of the day unless he and his mother were alone in the house, when he would come down and follow her everywhere, becoming increasingly clinging. When other members of the family were at home, he was resentful of their claims on her attention and he would then start being aggressive towards his mother; on several occasions he threw crockery across the kitchen, once just missing her face. His young brothers were visibly frightened; the whole family felt as if they were walking a tightrope. Meanwhile, Malcolm had refused to keep a follow-up appointment with the psychiatrist and caused such a scene over this that his mother was quite unable to do anything about it. She telephoned the doctor's secretary to explain what had happened.

It was twelve months after his parents had first begun to worry about Malcolm that his mother went to see the GP because she felt unable to cope much longer. She explained that he was obviously deeply unhappy but also angry. She found his behaviour threatening at times and she was worried about the way this was affecting her younger children. To her despair, the GP replied that she could do nothing further as Malcolm was not prepared to accept help; he was refusing to keep his outpatient appointments or to go to her surgery.

One evening a few weeks later, when his father was out, Malcolm threatened his mother, holding a bread knife to her throat, while his young brothers watched, screaming with fear. After a night of trauma, Malcolm was eventually persuaded by a doctor and a social worker to go into hospital on a voluntary basis.

On the ninth day after his admission to hospital Malcolm discharged himself. The distraught parents pleaded for someone to do something but they were told that Malcolm was 'not sectionable' following his short period of sanctuary and medication, as this had calmed him down. They would, however, keep a bed for him in case he would accept this. The parents' knowledge of Malcolm's recent history led them to believe that this could not happen, but when they put this to the hospital doctor, he shrugged, saying, 'Well, we'll see'. Once more, it seemed that the family was on its own.

Two months later, teachers called the parents to the school to express their concern about the welfare and progress of the two younger boys. Meanwhile, health professionals were now talking of Malcolm's *bad behaviour* rather than *illness* and asking the parents why they were prepared to put up with this?

Three weeks after the parents had gone to the school, Malcolm punched his mother in the face when she tried to persuade him to get out of bed to keep a new outpatient appointment. When she turned up at her GP's surgery, distraught and with a blackened eye, the doctor sympathized but told her 'you don't have to put up with this sort of behaviour, you know!'

That day, sick with worry over their two younger children, the parents finally gave up trying to care for Malcolm at home; they asked social workers, who had been suggesting something of the kind, to find lodgings for him and this was arranged. During the next eighteen months, his parents watched Malcolm gradually deteriorate further and further. He became thin and haggard with glazed, staring, eyes, and he showed no interest in his appearance or hygiene. After failing to pacify one outraged landlady after another, his now quite seriously depressed mother trekked the streets with Malcolm looking for new digs. Sometimes, the family sought the help of the police when Malcolm visited home and threatened his mother. Interestingly, the police acknowledged the nature of the family's plight and agreed the young man was sick, although professionals who worked with the mentally ill continued to deny this.

This sad phase in his life finished when Malcolm was discovered by police trying to set light to his lodgings. He was admitted to hospital under Section 2 of the Mental Health Act. Hospital staff quickly confirmed that the young man was suffering with a schizophrenic illness and he was at last given the appropriate treatment for his tormenting symptoms, together with the care he so badly needed.

Macolm had 'got into the system' three years after his parents first sought help for him. However, he was by this time seriously and, it seems, permanently damaged. With proper treatment for his illness, his delusional terrors faded quite quickly, together with the violence and hostility they had provoked, but years later Malcolm remains handicapped and in need of twenty-four hour care.

COMMENT

Malcolm's is a sad story with few, if any, redeeming features. It is worthy of note that caring professionals who have been involved in discussions about the events leading to Malcolm's eventual diagnosis and treatment, have been shocked and puzzled as to how he and his family could have received so little practical help. They have been quick to recognize several opportunities which should have been used to provide an effective service and they have been at a loss to know what else the parents could have done to obtain that service.

It might be a good idea to pause for a moment before going on to read the group's analysis to take a further look at what happened to Malcolm and his family and consider the following questions. At which points in this case could someone have intervened and ensured that Malcolm received the care and treatment he needed? Also, were the denials and resultant delays which took place caused by ignorance about psychosis or by a genuine desire to protect a very young person from a label of serious mental illness? If so would you want a son or daughter of yours to be 'protected' in this way?

GROUP'S ANALYSIS OF CASE STUDY

The main point which came up when the group discussed this case study was that although there were many signs of it, no-one seems to have considered at any time that Malcolm might have been suffering with schizophrenia. This omission was all the more disturbing because this illness is so common in this young age group (1).

Members decided to take a closer look to try and determine what it was that the many and various professionals in this case were trying to achieve.

The service provided by the GP

The group noted that the GP was receptive to the family's plea for help and later came to the conclusion that Malcolm was depressed and sought appropriate help for him. In this she appeared to have been the exception in recognizing he was mentally ill. However, when she didn't make any progress with the specialist team to whom she had referred her patient, the GP then backed off.

Everyone in the group felt that this doctor – as the only professional providing any continuity in the case – should have intervened later on when it became clear that something was seriously wrong. For example, at the point when the mother was on the verge of giving up, some of the group felt the GP should have arranged for a psychiatrist to visit the home and others felt she should have asked social workers to arrange a mental health assessment of her patient. However, no-one was in any doubt that the GP should have taken action at that point and that, later, when Malcolm punched his mother, the doctor should have made arrangements for his assessment for compulsory admission to hospital.

Members felt that despite the lack of effective backing she had received, the GP should have insisted on involving other professionals and getting them together to discuss this case and, equally important, she should have supported the parents rather than passing the buck back to them. Without the GP's support, they had nowhere to turn.

The service provided at the adolescent psychiatric unit

Group members were exasperated that this doctor and his team felt qualified to make an assessment of Malcolm without recourse to his past history or his parents' experience of the problem. Several pointed out that no-one seemed to be asking *why has Malcolm changed so dramatically?* The group had strong feelings about this. Surely, they insisted, when a young person's health is at stake, professionals should take the trouble to communicate properly with those who know him best? This couldn't happen, they insisted, in what they called a 'ward round situation' in which family members are invited to sit down amid a sea of new faces and are expected to ask and answer questions in front of their sick relative. Several members of the group had personal experience of this dilemma and had found it to be a very effective way of ensuring that relatives say nothing of consequence!

The family therapy sessions

Everyone felt that each of the family therapy sessions was a wasted opportunity to get to know what was really happening in this home and that this was great pity. There was some confusion in the group at this point as it seemed that the therapists came to their work with preconceived ideas which precluded their being able to empathize and identify with the parents' concerns. This was contrary to the group's understanding of the basis and aims of counselling work. Members were also confused as to why the therapists didn't follow up Malcolm's abrupt departure from the first session? Why, they asked, didn't his behaviour at this point give them any cause for concern? And, finally, they wanted to know, what was the aim of these sessions?

The sharing of a delusion?

Because most members 'had been there' themselves, it was taken for granted that the preconceived ideas of the staff team originated in Malcom's psychotic conviction that he was not ill and that the rest of the world (and most of all, those closest to him) had gone quite mad and were determined to lock him away. Not unnaturally, he would have desperately defended his position in order to keep the professionals at bay, telling them, perhaps, that his parents fussed too much, were too demanding and were cramping his style? If so, he was clearly successful in this.

But, one mother pointed out, 'this is such a familiar story; surely the experts have sussed it out by now?' But, no, other members were not convinced that this was so and a survivor pointed out that the all too frequent omission to 'sound out' those closest to the young person would seem to confirm these doubts. 'It's almost as if some health professionals prefer to collude with the sufferer's delusions!', she added ruefully.

Social workers and doctors qualified to work with the law

The group was surprised that, on at least two occasions, professionals working with the mental health law did not find grounds to section Malcolm when he was becoming a real threat to his mother. They believed he should not have been admitted to hospital voluntarily following the incident of holding a knife to his mother's throat. He had certainly proved himself to be a danger to others and his past record indicated that there was little chance he would comply with treatment if he were admitted to hospital on a voluntary basis and this, of course, proved to be the case.

A carer voiced the opinion that when Malcolm did in fact discharge himself from hospital, 'then he must surely have been sectionable *in the interests of his health*? He had been seen to be deteriorating in the recent past and, by keeping a bed for him, professionals were now acknowledging an unresolved *mental health problem*'. While the group agreed that this was a valid comment, several members pointed out that most professionals seemed to believe that a sufferer could not be sectioned *in the interests of his health*; instead they claimed that the individual had to be a danger to himself or others. Interestingly, the misunderstanding about this particular ground for sectioning is confirmed in the opening pages of the 1993 Code of Practice which draws attention to a widespread misconception on this point among professionals working with the mental health law (2).

The group discussed this reluctance, as they see it, of professionals to use the mental health legislation. They wished it was better understood that there is nothing so detrimental to a sufferer's future as leaving the individual unprotected and untreated rather than opting to use the law. This, in their opinion, amounted to neglect and they hoped there would come a time when this was generally recognized. A carer asked at this point about the actual role of professionals vis à vis *protecting someone who is vulnerable*, adding 'in Malcolm's case, the professionals were not taking on the responsibilities which give rise to their very existence'. A survivor agreed, saying that she believed that professionals have a responsibility to protect someone in these circumstances and she sometimes wondered what had happened to *old-fashioned caring*?

A duty to care?

This last comment brought the group back to a point which had already come up several times during this analysis; the plight of Malcolm's two young brothers — acknowledged, it seems, only by their parents and, later, their teachers. Members felt this was the sort of situation which should have concerned social workers; the children's needs should have been considered when Malcolm's behaviour became threatening. The group wanted to know if social workers qualified to use the mental health legislation (ASWs) and social workers who are involved in child-care liaise in such cases? 'Surely', a survivor commented, 'the ASW who assessed Malcolm the night he threatened his mother with a knife must have realized what was happening to these two children?' Others in the group felt this was a very important issue and they felt that surely the whole family's needs and welfare should influence decisions about whether or not someone should be sectioned?

They were, of course, quite right in this and the Code of Practice 1993 makes detailed reference to such matters (3).

Passing the buck?

Members noted that from the time that Malcolm discharged himself from hospital, he was suddenly being blamed for his own problems – the emphasis was no longer on 'bad parenting' but on his being 'bad' rather than 'mad'. Unfortunately, this, it seemed, put the onus back with the parents – again! It was up to them to 'do something' even if it meant turning their backs on their son.

This phenomenon was not new to group members. One member had been asked by a child psychiatrist, 'why don't you put him in care if you don't like the boy?', the boy being her sick son for whom she had been desperately seeking help. Why, she asked, angrily, do some professionals make suggestions which are 'contrary to all basic and natural parenting instincts?' Others in the group knew of similar examples, where families had been advised 'to turn out' a sick relative and they marvelled that this should be seen as an acceptable solution by some professionals. Someone wanted to know whether these same professionals would expect to be given such advice if they were seeking help for a sick son or daughter, and if so, whether they would act on it?

However, a survivor exclaimed, 'but, the question doesn't really arise, does it? Professionals who talk like this are just passing the buck!' On reflection, the rest of the group agreed that this probably summed up this vexing subject.

The police

Group members discussed the involvement of the police in this case. Most, but not everyone, felt that this was typical and that the police service has a reputation for acting as a safety-net for families seemingly deserted by the mental health services (4). One member commented 'it's amazing that with no mental health training, they can recognize serious mental illness' and two others felt that the the police have to work in the real world and see plenty of 'thugs' and 'lost causes' so they can more easily recognize someone who is pathetic and vulnerable like Malcolm.

Perhaps the most interesting comment on the role of the police in this context came from a relative who commented that, yes, the police come to these circumstances with considerable experience, 'but also without prejudice against the existence of mental illness...' After a long pause, the group came to the conclusion that this comment might be an important one, particularly as as other 'lay' members of the public such as family, friends, neighbours, shop-keepers and work colleagues also frequently recognize and acknowledge that someone is very ill before mental health professionals do so. They went on to talk about this and decided that this matter merited further attention (see *Exercise* at the end of the chapter).

The case analysis ended with the group as a whole expressing concern at the protracted delays which occurred before help was made available for Malcolm in view of the dangers which are so clearly inherent in delays in diagnosis and treatment (5). As we shall see, this matter came up again later. Not one group member involved in this analysis believed that Malcolm would now be so ill if he had received treatment at a much earlier stage and all felt this was a tragic waste of a young life. As someone put it, 'Well, yes, Malcolm slipped through the net, apparently surrounded by professionals!'.

THE WIDER PERSPECTIVE

How often do sufferers in their early or mid-teens suffer these sort of delays? Quite often, it seems; members cited four such further examples among their own families and friends.

Examples of similar delays

1. Considerable sums of public money were spent on this young sufferer in an attempt to resolve what were seen as her 'behaviour problems'. This went on for five years before the behaviour was recognized by the adult mental health services to be the natural outcome of an underlying schizophrenic illness. Her case study is featured in a later chapter.

2. This fourteen-year-old waited four years for an eventual diagnosis of schizophrenia. Meanwhile, a child psychiatrist decided that she was a 'gross personality disorder', although she had been a happy and stable child prior to suddenly becoming depressed, withdrawn and paranoid. The sufferer responded immediately she was given anti-psychotic treatment and has remained completely well for many years on a

maintenance dose of anti-psychotic medication. There has been no further mention of 'personality disorder', gross or otherwise!

3. A teenager with 'behaviourial problems' was treated by child psychiatrists for an 'adolescent crisis' for over four years. Eventually the sufferer was diagnosed as schizophrenic by the adult mental health services, after a long and gradual deterioration. 'This', the group member told us, 'was too late for this boy and his family. The torment and violence of this illness continues unabated to this day'.

4. Another young woman waited four years for a diagnosis of MD and appropriate treatment. Her case study features in a later chapter.

Why the delays?

Malcolm's case and these four further examples of young sufferers waiting so long for appropriate and effective help, raised questions about the quality and appropriateness of services available for young teenagers who may be developing a psychotic illness.

It was pointed out that as 80 per cent of all schizophrenia sufferers are actually diagnosed between the ages of 16 and 24 years of age, a significant minority must start their illness in the early and mid teens and yet in the cases being discussed not one had been appropriately diagnosed while under the supervision of the child psychiatric services. Problems tended to be put down to 'bad parenting' or to 'an adolescent crisis'. No mention had been made to any of these parents of even a possibility of there being an underlying serious mental illness in their child.

Perils of delays in treatment

There was a very strong feeling amongst the group that schizophrenia sufferers whose illness starts in the early and mid teens seem to fare rather more badly than other sufferers and that this might very well correlate with prolonged delays in diagnosing and treating their illness. All members were well aware that that untreated psychotic symptoms are bad news and that serious mental illness is no different from any other; the sooner it is treated the better!

A member of the group who has experienced schizophrenic breakdowns explained that she believes that problems are stored up for the future if the sufferer is left to live with delusional ideas for too long. These are so very real at the time that they still seem real in retrospect and can return at vulnerable moments, intruding on the individual's everyday life, raising doubts – particularly about important relationships – and threatening one's grip on reality. She summed this up with 'it's like having to rely on a distorted memory bank which can continue to play tricks on you'. She felt it was very possible that the delays that some very young sufferers had to cope with might stop them ever gaining insight into what part of their experience had been real and what had been illness. She felt very sad for them.

Another member could identify with this and pointed out that 'those of us who have MD may be more fortunate because first episodes are more common in the thirties and this precludes any confusion with adolescent disturbance. This might well facilitate earlier diagnosis and, in turn, partly explain the better prognosis so often associated with MD.'

Other members felt that all this made good sense and, whichever way you looked at it, delays in diagnosis and treatment in serious mental illness were bad news. They saw evidence of this too often to have any doubts on this matter.

SUMMING UP

In this chapter the LEAP group has looked at the predicament of a young sufferer subjected to long delays in obtaining a diagnosis and appropriate treatment. Members were concerned that other young new sufferers known to them seem to have been vulnerable to similar delays.

Other points which concerned them about this case were, first, a seeming reluctance by professionals to take responsibility for Malcolm's welfare, with a 'passing of the buck' back to the family at every stage of their involvement, and, second, a lack of evidence of caring amongst those who could have helped this sick young man and his family.

INFORMATION

The following pieces of information are relevant to points brought up during the group's analysis and discussion which have been highlighted in the text:

(1)　Age-group most likely to develop schizophrenia

One in every one hundred of us will develop a schizophrenic illness at some time in our lives but most sufferers – **80 per cent** – are, eventually, first diagnosed between 16 and 25 years of age. This means that for a significant minority the illness starts in the earlier teens.

(2)　Grounds for sectioning under the Mental Health Act 1983

One of the three grounds for compulsory admission to hospital is **'in the interests of the patient's health'**. However, as we have already noted, there is a widespread misconception that the individual has to present a danger to himself or other people. The Foreword of the 1993 Code of Practice comments:

'It has been widely reported that the criteria for admission to hospital under the Act have not not been correctly understood by all professionals. In particular, there is said to have been a misconception that patients may only be admitted under the Act if there is a risk to their own or other people's safety. In fact the Act provides for admission in the interests of the patient's health *or* of his or her safety, *or* for the protection of other people. This is also clearly spelt out in the new paragraph 2.6 of the Code.'

(3) The welfare of Malcolm's young brothers

Paragraph 2.9 of the 1993 Code of Practice is particularly relevant, i.e.:

Those assessing the patient must consider **the impact that any future deterioration or lack of improvement would have on relatives or close friends, especially those living with the patient.**

(4) The part played by the police in mental health crisis situations

Families frequently report that it is the police who have eventually responded to their unanswered pleas for help, for example:

(a)   An unpublished survey of 889 National Schizophrenia Fellowship members revealed that 161 sufferers obtained no help for their first episode of a serious mental illness until the police intervened (Mary Tyler 1986).

(b)   A National Schizophrenia Fellowship survey carried out on behalf of the Department of Health revealed that among the 563 carers who took part, the police were the most highly rated service when it comes to caring for the mentally ill, *Provision of Community Services for mentally ill people and their carers* (1990).

(5) The dangers in long delays in obtaining appropriate treatment

(a)   In a large extended study of first episodes of schizophrenia, Dr Tim Crow and his colleagues found the delay between onset of symptoms and admission to hospital to be a significant factor in predicting poor outcome in a schizophrenic illness. The most important determinant of relapse was duration of illness prior to starting neuroleptic medication. (Crow, T.J. *et al.* (1986) The Northwick Park Study of First Episodes of Schizophrenia, Part II: 'A randomized controlled trial of prophylactic neuroleptic treatment.' *British Journal of Psychiatry 148*, 120–7).

(b)   Richard Jed Wyatt has concluded, in his comprehensive overview of the use of neuroleptic medication and the natural course of schizophrenia, that 'some patients are left with a damaging residual if a psychosis is allowed to proceed unmitigated. While psychosis is undoubtedly demoralizing and stigmatizing, it may also be biologically toxic'. (Wyatt, R.J. 'Neuroleptics and the natural course of schizophrenia.' *Schizophrenia Bulletin*, 17, 2, 1991).

EXERCISE

As we noted earlier in this chapter, when the LEAP group looked at the role that the police often play in helping families trying to obtain help for a sick relative, one member commented that the police come to these crisis situations '*without prejudice against the existence of mental illness*'. When discussing this comment, members pointed out that other 'lay' members of the public – such as family, friends, neighbours, shop-keepers and work colleagues – frequently recognize serious mental illness in a sufferer before mental health professionals appear to do so. In view of this frequently observed phenomenon and the now widely acknowledged dangers of delaying treatment in a psychotic illness, the LEAP group felt it had to be worth considering this further and decided that the exercise for this chapter should focus on the following question:

Is it possible that the professional training and day-to-day experience of those who work with serious mental illness might prejudice their natural skills in recognizing abnormal behaviour in another human being?

CHAPTER 6

Another young sufferer slipping in and out of the system

As we noted in the last chapter, there may be no recognition or acknowledgement of serious mental illness while new sufferers are still in their early or mid teens. Let's take a look at what this has meant for one young woman and her family.

CASE STUDY

Her parents had not found Kay to be an easy child; she was very sensitive and yet particularly prone to upsetting other children and getting into trouble at school. Fortunately, however, she was relatively cheerful and contented in the security of her home and got on well enough with her parents and older brother.

Things suddenly worsened towards the end of Kay's first year in senior school when she started to complain of being bullied in the playground, particularly at lunchtime. Although her mother agreed to her coming home for lunch to minimize the opportunity for bullying, Kay's behaviour quickly deteriorated and she became quite abusive towards her parents; it seemed that they could do nothing right for her. She kept blaming them for sending her to a state school, insisting that they should have paid for her to go to a local private school with two of her former classmates. Every family mealtime was spoilt by Kay going over this again and again, refusing to eat most of her meal and then storming out of the room as noisily as she could.

When her parents sought help from the school about the bullying and explained that this was causing problems at home as well, the head teacher arranged for an educational psychologist to spend some time with Kay. As a result of this, the whole family was referred to the local child guidance clinic several weeks later.

One way and another, this referral seemed to produce nothing but problems for the family. Kay's normally placid and easy-going brother was not at all happy about having to miss a once-weekly double games lesson to attend family sessions at the clinic and soon opted out of these. His parents found this to be a quite natural and acceptable decision but were dismayed to find that this was seen at the clinic to be some sort of failure on their part. In fact, the parents quickly realized that the psychiatrist conducting the family sessions considered most of Kay's problems to be caused by them too. He told them at one point that they did not like Kay and were projecting their own problems on to her; she had become a scapegoat for the conflict within their marriage. When, surprised and hurt, they queried this, he told them that this conflict was clearly evident when they argued at these sessions about the best way to cope with their younger daughter.

Kay's parents had certainly started to argue on this subject. Her behaviour at home was becoming increasingly difficult and she would hurl abuse at them for days after each family session, going over and over each and every word either of her parents had said in the last session and making it clear that she found their comments personal and a betrayal of some sort. What with Kay's reaction to anything they said at the clinic and the doctor's reaction to any conflict which arose during these sessions, the parents quickly learned to say very little at all. In any event, it seemed that they couldn't win. When they reported that Kay had cut up all her father's ties after one session and, after the next one, she had poured bleach over their best carpet, they were given to understand by the doctor that they were over-reacting. Similarly, when they brought up the matter of Kay being bullied, they were told they were projecting problems within the family onto the school.

Some months after the referral to the child guidance clinic, the parents decided to go along with Kay's constant demands to move from her present school, where the bullying had continued unabated, to the smaller private school down the road. For a while, things improved and the family had some peace at home but before long she was complaining of bullying again and was also getting into a lot of trouble with the teachers at the school, who were alarmed by her destructive and irrational behaviour. Towards the end of her second term at the new school, the headmaster sent for Kay's parents and advised them that he and his staff could no longer cope with their daughter's bizarre and vandalizing behaviour.

Before they left the school, one of the teachers drew the parents aside to say they had previously seen this sort of behaviour in two other children and they had each turned out to be mentally ill. Their subsequent attempts to discuss this with their GP and with the doctor at the child guidance clinic came to nothing. Instead, the education authority was asked to arrange for Kay to be sent away to a school for maladjusted children and she spent much of the rest of her childhood at this and a further institution. This supposed solution to her problems was achieved at considerable public expense while inflicting acute distress and feelings of guilt on the parents and prolonged suffering for Kay herself. She remembers these years with horror and talks about them incessantly.

At 17 years, Kay returned home. She blamed her parents for all that had happened to her and spent most her time raging at them, repeating herself again and again. Meanwhile, her behaviour was also repetitive and ritualistic. Things got worse in the evenings, when Kay was particularly restless and convinced she was in danger of an attack of some sort. She was terror-stricken and up and about most of the night. She was clearly unwell and her GP referred the young woman to the adult mental health services. As a result of this a psychiatrist told Kay he wanted to help her and felt she should be admitted to hospital. Predictably, Kay wanted nothing to do with this but, after several appointments with the same psychiatrist, she finally agreed to his suggestion.She was quickly assessed as having a schizophrenic illness and given appropriate treatment.

Despite being prescribed quite heavy doses of anti-psychotic medication, Kay's illness did not respond as well as had been hoped, although the incessant and tortuous racing of her mind calmed down and this in itself brought her and her family some respite. Nevertheless, evenings were still difficult and sometimes Kay seemed hell-bent on finding trouble late at night. There were several incidents when she was accused of vandalizing local property, although more often than not she would be destructive within the family home.

Several professionals in the community were now involved with Kay but before very long they were telling the parents that their daughter had a 'personality disorder' which was clearly more important than any illness she might, or might not, have. The parents started to feel they were on their own again, chasing around after their desperate daughter trying to keep her on the right side of the law.

After a year or so of this, by which time Kay's name had become legend with local professionals, a sympathetic social worker referred the young woman to an informal centre which specialized in supporting young people, most of whom had to cope with a serious mental illness. Perhaps because she was so restless – almost hyperactive – in her efforts to escape from her tormenting thoughts, Kay turned up at the centre several times over the next couple of months and stayed just long enough each time for the staff-team to form an opinion about her which was at odds with the reports of behaviour problems which had accompanied her referral. They were alarmed by the mixture of terror and smouldering fury they sensed in the girl. They were equally impressed by the fact that – almost unheard of – some of their regular clients were frightened enough to avoid her, convinced she was quite dangerously mad.

When the psychiatrist who had given Kay a diagnosis of schizophrenia received the centre's report, he persuaded her to come into hospital again. This time he tried a newly available anti-psychotic drug which had a dramatic effect on Kay's illness. The young woman's torment abated and this time everyone could see the improvement in her. By the time Kay was discharged, she had been stabilized on the medication and arrangements had been made for her to see the psychiatrist regularly, to have a community psychiatric nurse (CPN) visit her fortnightly and to attend the centre where the staff had realized that there was something seriously wrong with her.

By now, Kay was able to talk about the intolerable tension she had suffered when her thoughts tormented her and how she could only cope with her terror by attacking cars and property instead of obeying the constant messages that she should go out and viciously hurt some living creature. She never acknowledged hearing 'voices' and always referred to her thoughts 'going round and round in my head, planning these ghastly things'. The young woman continued to display repetitive behaviour but the only lingering symptom which still upset her were 'these thoughts which come into my head' accompanied by feelings of shame and guilt that she should have them. Staff at the centre encouraged Kay to talk about these feelings of guilt when she couldn't cope with them – when she was convinced she was wicked – and gradually she appreciated that this might not be the case.

Now just out of her teens, Kay had few of the social skills of her peers but as she became more well so she gained a reputation for co-operating with everyone who tried to help her and for being particularly relaxed and sensitive with young children and animals. In particular – and a real plus for the whole family – Kay was now relating well to her parents and seeking their company much of the time. Mercifully, too, the vandalizing had stopped! Whereas Kay hadn't attained anything like a normal lifestyle for a young woman of her age, she found new contentment both at home and at the centre where she knew she was among friends.

This relatively ideal situation continued for over three years until, suddenly, Kay announced that she was coming off her medication. She would not listen when everyone – including fellow clients at the centre – told her this could be dangerous. All she would say was that she *had* to come off the medication and would do this gradually. Before long, Kay could be seen to be deteriorating dramatically. She was also starting to vandalize her parents' home again. However, when they pleaded with professionals for something to be done for their daughter, they were told that she couldn't be forced to take medication.

A year or so later, Kay was in and out of court frequently and mental health professionals were talking about her being 'bad rather than mad'; first and foremost a 'personality disorder'. Her exhausted parents are now hoping that she is not going to slip through the net again.

COMMENT

In this case we find some of the same problems faced in the last chapter by Malcolm and his family and in particular more evidence of long delays in 'getting into the system' for these very young new sufferers.

It might be a good idea to pause at this point and consider whether or not you feel that Kay's original referral was handled properly and that it was a wise decision to send her away from home? Whichever way you feel about this, make a few notes to back up your opinion and follow this up by noting any viable alternatives which you feel might have been considered.

GROUP'S ANALYSIS OF CASE STUDY

The thing that struck LEAP group members most about Kay's story was that here was another case of a young sufferer 'slipping through the net' right at the start of her illness, while the parents were blamed for their child's problems.

A problem specific to young sufferers?

The similarity of the start of Kay's story to Malcolm's, and to others known to the group, again provoked questions by members about the appropriateness of the child psychiatry services for young teenagers who may be developing a serious mental illness. One carer summed this up with, 'the doctor obviously did not think such a young girl *could* be mentally ill'. A survivor agreed with this observation and felt this was an inexcusable assumption, adding, 'quite apart from the problems in the home that the family was reporting, Kay was referred to the clinic because she was experiencing difficulties at school. Later, the second school found these to be very real and the problems were also getting worse by the day at home'. Why, this member wanted to know, was there no straightforward psychiatric assessment made at this point? If nothing came of it, that was fine and no harm would have been done.

Other members agreed that, yes, this sort of assessment should be mandatory in this type of situation.

Judgement rather than communication

Members marvelled that, 'once again, the parents were judged rather than listened to' and a survivor felt this was very worrying. 'Surely', she said, 'it must be very intimidating for parents to be told by the experts that it's their fault?' Yes, indeed; other members felt quite strongly about this. And they are not alone in this; among others, a leading brain scientist has pointed out just how devastating it is for parents to try to cope with being blamed for a serious mental illness in their child (1).

A lack of listening

Someone in the group protested 'but instead of making judgements, psychiatrists should listen to the parents; they know their child'. This was the general feeling within the group. Several members marvelled at the lack of interest at the clinic when Kay's parents reported that she was taking out her feelings on them after each visit there by doing things like cutting up all her father's ties and pouring bleach on a best carpet. Several members laughed when someone suggested that it almost beggared belief that parents could be told they were over-reacting in such circumstances. They were fairly sure that neither they, nor most other parents they knew, would be able to cope with this sort of outrage in their homes – emotionally or financially!

Perhaps more significantly, one carer pointed out that the psychiatrist missed Kay's cries for help as the child knew these outrages would inevitably be reported to him. In other words, she was making it quite clear to all concerned what the family sessions were doing to her, wasn't she?

Echoes of the old family theories

Meanwhile, a survivor wondered why some professionals seem to confuse the tension they find in families trying to cope with an undiagnosed psychotic illness in their midst with some assumed pre-existing conflict within the home? Others in the group were bemused by this phenomenon too, but felt it all came back to a lack of interest in listening to what relatives had to say about how things used to be *before* they needed to seek help.

However, several members in the group felt that such dangerous assumptions were based on the old family theories, leading to ideas that the child with the problems was being *scapegoated* by the rest of a 'disfunctioning family' (2). One carer, a mother, was amazed that anyone could think like this. Didn't they realize, she asked, that one of the cruellest parts of watching this type of illness in your child is having to compare their fate with that of their brothers and sisters?

This question provoked real emotion in several parents in the group. One said firmly that 'scapegoating' was a very ugly word in this context and another said quietly, 'not only do I feel guilty if I go out and find I'm enjoying myself, knowing that my son can't – sometimes I even resent it when his brothers do'. Unusually for members of the LEAP group, there was a long pause after this carer's barely audible statement until another mother thanked her, quite emotionally, for voicing this raw feeling that she had always felt was hers alone until that moment.

Others in the group joined in the discussion at this point and this led to members marvelling how anyone could fail to recognize or identify with the pain of parents watching a sick child suffer? A survivor summed it up with 'it's as if some professionals can hide behind a theory; it can distance them from the feelings and the pain confronting them. I think this is very worrying!'

Going down the wrong road

Members went on to discuss the decision to send Kay away for the rest of her childhood, with her parents rendered impotent to do anything about this. One carer summed up the general feeling at this stage with, 'If Kay had had appropriate treatment at the time that the teacher recognized she was ill, then she could have been protected from further deterioration and avoided some nightmare years'.

A 'precarious' diagnosis

No-one was surprised that Kay's illness had only partially responded to medication the first time round, but they were concerned that this then led to doubts that the diagnosis was correct. More specifically, she even started to 'slip out of the system' again, with suggestions being made that she had personality problems rather than an illness. A survivor said, yes, she had noticed before that 'whereas initially the parents may be blamed for their child's behaviour, later on, if the medication doesn't work, then it's the sufferer who's at fault!' Other members were interested in this comment as it certainly seemed to apply to Malcolm (in Chapter 5) and now to Kay. 'But', one carer exclaimed, 'this is not good enough after these young people have been through so much. This is the time when the doctors should persevere and then persevere some more!'

Members emphatically agreed with this last comment and noted that this had not been the case with Kay until a social worker had taken pity on the family and had referred Kay to a centre where the staff had recognized that something was seriously wrong. In other words, it seemed to have been chance that had led to Kay getting back into the system. As one carer pointed out, it was the concerned reports of the centre staff which had given the psychiatrist an incentive (or renewed confidence in his original diagnosis, perhaps?) to persevere with finding the right treatment for his patient.

A welcome but precarious respite

The group was pleased to learn about the enthusiastic support Kay received at the centre and from the CPN team. Also, members were encouraged to know that the psychiatrist not only saw his patient frequently but welcomed her parents along to these sessions. Members could not see that more support could be provided for any sufferer but they wondered why it seemed to evaporate at just the time she needed it most. A survivor asked 'couldn't something have been done – couldn't a united front of professionals and carers have helped to change Kay's mind about coming off medication at this early stage?' Others in the group felt that this must have been worth a try and, at the very least, this would have given those involved an opportunity to pool ideas as to how to deal with this crisis. As it was, it seemed to members that all the support was given arbitrarily rather than as part of a programme to prevent a vulnerable patient from further relapse, and this didn't make any sense to them.

Grounds for sectioning

All members felt that with this young woman's history and improved quality of life on anti-psychotic medication over the past three years, there was every reason to suppose that she would deteriorate when she came off this. A carer pointed out that when this indeed started to happen, then she could have been sectioned 'in the interests of her health' (3). The group had noted when discussing Malcolm in the last chapter that there was a widespread assumption among professionals that a sufferer has to be a danger to themselves or others before they can be sectioned (4) but this didn't alter the fact that the law not only provides for sectioning 'in the interests of patient's health' but that it was the only course left open to professionals wanting to protect Kay from further damage. Members couldn't understand why someone who had been so ill for so long could be allowed to relapse in this way. As one put it, 'surely the system owed it to Kay and her family to do something?'

THE WIDER PERSPECTIVE

The first topic which the group returned to at this point was the vexed subject of 'labelling'. They just could not understand why terms such as 'personality disorder' could be so freely used while many professionals abhorred the use of words such as manic depression and schizophrenia. As one carer pointed out, 'Psychosis is treatable but a 'personality disorder' isn't!' and a survivor nodded, saying that sufferers themselves invariably see 'personality disorder' as being a derogatory label anyway. She really felt that some well-meaning individuals tended to lose the plot when they got onto the subject of labelling!

A carer was particularly concerned with another aspect of this subject; 'I worry that this is a way of removing those sufferers who are difficult to treat from the system – another way of passing the buck'. He pointed out that the mental health legislation doesn't allow for sectioning someone with a personality disorder if doctors claim that the individual will not benefit from treatment (5). This could preclude sufferers labelled as 'personality order' from getting help in a crisis; it could put them outside the jurisdiction of the mental health legislation. His concern may well be justified as research has revealed that individuals whose schizophrenic illness is, in fact, treatable can slip through the net this way (6). The group felt that here was another reason to obtain an accurate diagnosis as soon as possible and then to make sure it is not taken away later!

A disadvantaged cycle

Meanwhile, there was a general feeling within the group that the risk of falling by the wayside was particularly strong for young sufferers like Kay, who may have initially endured years of waiting for a diagnosis and treatment. Apart from anything else, these delays could very much influence whether or not their illness would respond to treatment. 'Then,' a survivor commented, 'instead of recognizing this as an inevitable result of all the delays, everyone starts to doubt again that the individual is ill. 'Yes,' someone agreed, 'it's a vicious circle, really, isn't it?' This was how other members saw it too; it seemed to them as if the battle with a serious mental illness had been lost for some young sufferers from the word 'go'.

A need to break this cycle

Members came to the conclusion that the system had a special responsibility to recognize the plight of these young sufferers whose illness may be difficult to treat after long delays in being diagnosed. As one member had said earlier in this discussion, doctors need to persevere – and persevere some more – with the Kays of this world. There was a general feeling that (a) such cases should be singled out for special attention at times of pending crisis, making it easier for professionals to feel they can take preventive action and that (b) the sufferer should also remain the responsibility of one psychiatrist. As one mother put it, 'Perhaps this way, the system can do something to make up for the disadvantage that Kay and other young people suffer through no fault of their own'.

The young sufferer's special vulnerability

At this point, members returned to their primary concern with Malcolm's case in the last chapter. Several members of the group wondered if professionals working in child psychiatry are alert to the sort of numbers they might expect among their young teenage referrals whose problems may well be due to a developing serious mental illness? Others wondered whether there is adequate training anyway in recognizing the signs and symptoms of this type of illness? One carer said that the name of one particular child psychiatrist, who had completely misread her son's problem, came up so often when she talked with other mothers with a similar experience that she wondered if doctors like him ever received any feedback on what happened to their patients after they were referred to the adult mental health service? Once more, members were addressing the question of feedback and suspecting there was little of this where the handling of serious mental illness was concerned.

A research project

Bearing this in mind, members felt that it might be a useful exercise for someone to set up a research project to determine how often longstanding problems of young people referred during their teens do in fact turn out to be caused by an undiagnosed psychotic illness. It seemed to members that there may well be a case for highlighting the vulnerability of these very young sufferers, particularly if they are subjected to the sort of delays which can later make their illness difficult to treat.

SUMMING UP

In this chapter, the group has looked at a second teenager who barely got into the system before slipping out of it again. They were sad to find that this young woman and her parents now seem to have come full circle, despite her having made considerable progress for several years on anti–psychotic medication.

Members suggested that research might be justified, to investigate just how often teenage sufferers have similar experiences to Kay and Malcolm and other young people known to the LEAP group. They felt this might highlight the need to set up specialized screening for referrals in this age group and that any extra resources needed for this could be demonstrated to be cost–effective. Meanwhile, members felt that these young people should be regarded as especially vulnerable in later years if they are to be protected from further damage and finally falling by the wayside.

INFORMATION

The following pieces of information are relevant to points brought up during the group's analysis and discussion which have been highlighted in the text:

(1)   Blaming of parents

Colin Blakemore has commented 'to lose a child to schizophrenia is a tremendous load to bear. To be told that this awful disorder is due to the way the child was nurtured is far worse.'

(*The Mind Machine* (1988), London: BBC Books, p.124.)

(2)   Alleged scapegoating of sufferers

See the present author's *The Reality of Schizophrenia* (1991), Faber and Faber, p.80, for a discussion on this particular aspect of one of the discredited 'family theories'.

(3)   Sectioning in the interests of the patient's health

The *1993 Code of Practice* on the Mental Health Act 1983 makes it clear that the Act allows for the sectioning of a patient 'in the interests of his health' – see the Foreword, last paragraph on page iii and also that this point is reiterated in paragraph 2.6 of the Code on page 4.

(4)   A widespread misconception

The *1993 Code of Practice* on the Mental Health Act 1983 states that:

'It has been widely reported that the criteria for admission to hospital under the Act have not been correctly understood by all professionals. In particular, there is said to have been a misconception that patients may only be admitted under the Act if there is a risk to their own or other people's safety. In fact the Act provides for admission in the interests of the patient's health, *or* of his or her safety, *or* for the protection of other people (see Foreword, page iii).'

(5)　The 'treatability' clause

The Mental Health Act 1983 states that:

> 'An application for treatment may be made in respect of a patient on the ground that… (b) in the case of psychopathic disorder…such treatment is likely to alleviate or prevent a deterioration of his condition (Part II, Section 3, see p.3).'

Thus if a psychiatrist claims that an individual with a psychopathic disorder (which includes 'personality disorder') will not benefit from treatment, then that individual is not provided for in this part of the mental health legislation, unless and until such time as another doctor thinks differently.

(6)　Abuse of the 'treatability' clause?

An interesting and comprehensive survey, carried out by a forensic psychiatrist, demonstrated that many of the individuals recommended by the courts for psychiatric treatment who are refused admission to hospital on the basis of a label of 'personality disorder', have nevertheless improved with neuroleptic drug treatment; in other words they have a treatable schizophrenic illness. This study of mentally abnormal men remanded to Winchester Prison revealed that when the courts have tried to refer such men for hospital treatment:

> 'On a conservative estimate, one in five prisoners on remand were rejected for treatment. These generally were the men most in need of care and exhibiting the severest degree of social impairment. The majority of those rejected were suffering from schizophrenia (Coid, J. (1988) 'Rejected or accepted by the National Health Service', *British Medical Journal 296*, 25 June).'

Thus, it seems, a label of 'personality disorder' can be used as an excuse to refuse treatment. At the time of writing this label has come into everyday use and it may be especially important to bear the 'treatability' clause in mind.

EXERCISE

Imagine you have been seconded by the Department of Health to produce a plan which would ensure that young teenage sufferers obtained assessment, treatment and care from the earliest possible time. You have jurisdiction over the various disciplines involved but you have been cautioned that little extra funding will be made available. Detail your recommendations.

CHAPTER 7

Into the system, yet falling by the wayside

We have looked at several examples of delays which can take place over 'getting into the system' and at others where the individual seems to teeter on the edge of the system. Jane's experience is different; she is one of those sufferers who receive a diagnosis and treatment in time to make a promising recovery, only to then slip through the net.

CASE STUDY

At 21 years of age Jane had a psychotic breakdown. Previously she had become involved with a group of youngsters experimenting with street drugs and had later gone to live with them a mile or so away from the family home. Her parents now know that Jane had been taking cannabis for some time before the move.

In the months leading up to her breakdown, Jane complained of a succession of obscure and rather bizarre physical complaints, all of which the family GP took seriously. However, each investigation carried out at the local hospital came to nothing and merely led on to Jane presenting a new and different problem. Later, it was noticeable that all of these physical problems faded when the young woman's psychosis was successfully treated in hospital.

Jane quickly became well and was discharged from hospital to the family home after a month or so. She was offered support at a drop-in centre for young people with a serious mental illness and also allocated a nurse (CPN) to keep an eye on her because there was some remaining concern about the young woman's recent drug habit.

It was noted at the centre that Jane had exceptional artistic talent, together with a buoyant, excitable personality. The staff also gained the impression that although she seemed to be very well, the young woman had little insight into her illness. Jane was dismissive of her psychiatrist's firm advice to persevere with a maintenance dose of medication. She had not used cannabis since going into hospital and declared that she wanted to be free of all drugs, albeit cannabis or medication. The centre staff's concern about Jane's reluctance to persevere with medication was shared with the newly appointed CPN.

Meanwhile, it was very clear that Jane could not wait to get on with her life and, in particular, to get a job. She was very determined about this and she quickly found herself voluntary work with elderly people. She immediately stopped attending the centre and just popped in and out with excited progress reports. She was loving her work and within a few months her enthusiastic efforts were rewarded and her employer offered the young woman paid work on a trial basis. The job could eventually lead to her being trained for a longed-for career and Jane was naturally delighted with the progress she had made.

When she had successfully completed her six-months probationary period at work, Jane moved out of the parental home again; this time to live with a work colleague she had been dating for some time. Her parents were not too happy about the move at this time as Jane had recently come off her medication despite the warnings she had received from her mother and the CPN about the possible consequences of doing this too soon. The parents were also concerned that Jane's new partner almost certainly knew nothing about her breakdown. The young woman said she considered this to be of no consequence although she had carefully hidden the information from her employer.

Very soon after the move, her parents noted that Jane was talking about having all sorts of physical symptoms again and, more worrying, she was also complaining that people at work were talking about her behind her back. About this time, it became clear too that Jane was going to some lengths to avoid her mother. One way and another, things seemed to be going wrong again and the parents wished they could talk with Jane's partner, but they didn't feel they could intrude on her personal life in this way.

However, her mother did approach the CPN team to find out how the nurse who had been supporting Jane now felt about her progress. She was told that as Jane had moved and was doing so well in her job, this had seemed a good time to acknowledge that she didn't need specialist help any longer, so no-one was monitoring her. However, when they heard about the parents' worries, it was agreed that a new nurse would contact Jane and, hopefully, keep an eye on things for a while.

Still worried, Jane's mother approached the family GP, who was quite willing to discuss her daughter with her. He confirmed he was sending Jane to the hospital for similar investigations to those carried out previously. He did not share her mother's feeling that a whole range of physical problems had heralded Jane's breakdown, only to resolve themselves when she was given anti-psychotic medication. He did not think it was 'all happening again', as her mother suggested, and made it clear that he felt she was being over-anxious about her daughter's welfare because of the young woman's recent illness.

Jane's mother certainly was very anxious and she eventually telephoned the psychiatrist who had supervised Jane's treatment during her breakdown. He was sympathetic and said he would talk with his colleagues and consider whether or not a domiciliary visit was called for.

By now, Jane was ignoring her mother, but not her father. She met up with him several times during those weeks in which his wife was trying to obtain help from professionals. He realized that his daughter was taking frequent sick leave and agreed with his wife that things were going downhill fast. He also suspected that Jane was taking cannabis again, although she emphatically denied this.

Her father was not surprised to learn the next time he saw Jane that her employer had sent her home on sick leave as she had insisted that she was so physically ill that she couldn't stand for more than a few minutes at a time while doing her work. Not long afterwards, her father learned that Jane had had to attend for a medical assessment which had resulted in her employer being told that Jane had recently suffered with a psychotic breakdown. Having deliberately withheld this information, she was immediately dismissed.

Now, of course, Jane's partner also knew about her medical history. It was not long before he made contact with the parents, saying he could not cope any longer with Jane's wild accusations; she was paranoid about him and determined that he was unfaithful to her. He now realized that her continued complaints about her mother were also based on paranoia. She had refused to see her psychiatrist when he called at the house. She had leaned out of a window and showered insults and threats on him. The specialist had left and they had heard nothing since, although that was over a week ago. He now knew that Jane had similarly dispensed with a CPN's offer of support a few weeks earlier. In short, Jane's partner had no intention of throwing her out on the street but wanted to know if she could go back and live with her parents? He felt quite unable to cope with her behaviour and he also felt cheated because Jane had not told him about her breakdown.

Her parents were quite prepared for Jane to return home and hoped this might make it simpler to get help for her. As it turned out, however, Jane had no intention of returning to live with her parents at this time; she would still have nothing to do with her mother and was determined to 'go it alone'. She found herself lodgings but within a couple of months she had moved again. Her father visited his daughter several times, watching helplessly as the situation worsened. He was at a loss to know how much she was influenced by the cannabis she now admitted she was taking 'occasionally' and how much her behaviour was due to the return of her illness. He and his wife continued to seek help but it seemed that none of the professionals who might have provided this were able to make any meaningful contact with their daughter, saying she refused their offers of help. When the mother tried to contact the psychiatrist again, his secretary told her that Jane had been verbally abusive and threatening to the doctor and had written to the health authority about him. That, it seemed, was that!

One morning the parents woke up to find that friends of Jane had given her a lift to a commune somewhere up north. Beyond knowing she had arrived there safely, they heard nothing more for ten months, when she turned up on their doorstep one evening, tense and high. Her mother later described the next 48 hours as like walking on broken glass, with Jane defensive and smouldering with anger; 'ready to blow at any time', as her father put it. Her parents made Jane as welcome as they could and quickly learned that even innocuous queries were resented. They resisted an almost overwhelming temptation to ask more questions and although they gathered she may have walked out on the commune they learned nothing more about their daughter's lifestyle.

Two nights later Jane was gone, as abruptly as she had arrived. Her parents now felt more helpless than ever. They could only hope that their unintrusive welcome had prepared the way for Jane to return soon and some months later she did turn up again, desperately ill. Three nightmare days later, Jane was sectioned and back in the system at last.

As her paranoid hostility faded with treatment, Jane was soon reunited with her parents and returned home to live with them. Nevertheless, twelve months later, although she now has more insight into her illness and has not abused street drugs since her second breakdown, Jane has made nothing like the sort of recovery she made after the first episode of her illness. She is frustrated that she is not well enough to work and frequently has bouts of quite severe depression alternating with agitated restlessness.

COMMENT

Jane is one of those young sufferers whose appearance and presentation seem to militate against their future welfare. Like Marie in Chapter 3, she is attractive, bright and lucid and it does seem that these are not characteristics which many mental health workers connect with serious mental illness. Perhaps this was why it was assumed that Jane was well enough to get on with the rest of her life when she demonstrated she was able to do all the things most of us take for granted, for example getting and holding down a job, finding a partner and moving away from the parental home. However, she was only able to do all these 'ordinary' things while her psychosis was kept at bay.

In retrospect, there were several factors in Jane's case which might have signalled that she was especially vulnerable. In view of this, it might be worthwhile to pause for a moment to go through this case study again and to make a note of any factors which you feel could have put this apparently well young woman at risk.

GROUP'S ANALYSIS OF CASE STUDY

The general feeling of the group about Jane's story was one of frustration that this potentially well young woman slipped through the net. As one mother put it, 'Jane seemed so well that they let her drop out of the system'. Others in the group found it strange that those working with serious mental illness could have so much faith in such a lightning recovery. They felt there were obvious danger signals which should have alerted everyone to Jane's vulnerability.

A lack of insight

Members felt that the staff-team at the centre which Jane attended so briefly had appreciated Jane was vulnerable when they had noted her apparent lack of insight into what had happened to her. They also noted her consequent dismissive attitude about taking medication and alerted her CPN to this. A survivor, who has had several breakdowns herself, felt that convincing Jane that she needed medication indefinitely should have occurred in hospital. 'There is not enough said about "preventive" medication; about staying on this to keep well', she added.

Others in the group agreed with this comment; Jane had been discharged when she was seemingly bright and well but she had not made the excellent recovery she was credited with because she did not appreciate her vulnerability to relapse in the future. In fact, she was frantically busy rushing around convincing herself that none of this had happened to her and she succeeded in making most of the people around her think that she was doing fine, thank you!

A previous drug habit

The group felt that Jane's recent drug habit could have made her especially vulnerable. Members pointed out that drug abuse is bad news in individuals with a serious mental illness and particularly so if they persevered with the habit (1). It seemed to them that this was largely overlooked by professionals when she appeared to be so well.

A carer pointed out that it should have been clear that the chances that Jane might abuse drugs again were increased once her symptoms were no longer controlled by medication. She and other members felt this was one particularly good reason for those involved in her case to have been more concerned about Jane's coming off the medication. 'Yes', this called for 'more persuasion from all the professionals concerned before things had gone too far', as another carer put it.

Coming off medication

This brought members to the point which surprised them most about this case. They did not understand how a premature decision to come off medication against the advice of her mother and her CPN could have led the CPN team to assume Jane needed no further monitoring, particularly when she also moved out of the relative security of the family home.

Members had noted in other case studies a tendency for patients to be lost to the system when they move and this seemed to them to be a 'symptom' of a lack of co-ordination within the services. In Jane's case, it seemed that she did not even move out of the district served by the first CPN's team and members wondered why there was no continuity at this point, particularly as the CPN had been concerned about her giving up her medication? As one of the group, a survivor herself, pointed out, 'patients coming off medication need to be followed up thoroughly. Often their relapse is not evident to professionals for a long time after stopping the medication and I don't think professionals are always aware that total relapse might take months rather than weeks.'

A need to listen

This brought the group back to a subject which has cropped up in most of the cases they have analyzed; the importance of listening to those who know the sufferer best. They were not surprised that Jane's mother was the first to notice that her daughter was relapsing again but they were exasperated that she and her husband had to rush around trying to make professionals listen to them. Furthermore, they really got nowhere at all with this, insofar as obtaining effective help for their daughter was concerned. Members felt this was quite unacceptable and a mother in the group exclaimed 'listening to the people who know and love the sufferer is so important. They want their loved one to be well and happy – they won't just make up the scenario for the fun of it!'

Another carer felt that the weak point in this case was that 'professionals did not take responsibility for the illness and its effects'. This, he pointed out, was not the same as taking responsibility away from Jane or her parents, it was all about professionals using their expertise and resources to protect a sufferer from the worst effects of a serious mental illness. They had unwittingly turned their backs on the sufferer who was now too ill to take that responsibility but the parents took over at that point and did everything they could to get help for her, including alerting everyone concerned as to what was happening. At this point, he believed that the professionals should have taken back the responsibility for protecting Jane. Members agreed with this viewpoint and decided to take a closer look at how professionals responded to the mother's pleas for help.

The CPN team

The nursing team arranged for a second CPN to call on Jane, but, the group asked, was this likely to be a viable solution? Members thought not; they weren't surprised that Jane was not prepared to let a new CPN into her life at this stage, and certainly not at her partner's home. Anyway, it did not seem appropriate for a stranger to attempt to assess Jane when a colleague had previous experience of her. Members felt that an invitation from the first CPN to meet up somewhere mutually acceptable might have been more productive. Whereas such a meeting may not have influenced Jane in any way, this CPN could at least have assessed her and reported back on any deterioration she found in her former client.

The GP

It seemed to the group that it was a great pity that this doctor was sensitive enough to talk with an 'anxious mother' about her daughter but was not prepared to hear what she was saying. Members knew of other cases where sufferers turn up regularly at their GP's surgery with one physical ailment after another without revealing their real problem; the inner torment which precedes a psychotic breakdown. Interestingly, an article in the *British Medical Journal* in 1993 (2) warned doctors about this phenomenon but, perhaps because each surgery has so few cases of psychotic illness, the message may not be getting through.

The psychiatrist

This doctor's reaction to Jane's dilemma caused some real concern among group members. They were at a loss to understand why, after responding sympathetically to her mother and then acting upon what she had to say, he then took to his heels because his patient shouted abuse at him and went on to report him to the health authority. 'Surely', exclaimed a survivor, 'this wasn't the patient he remembered when he discharged her from hospital? Surely, her behaviour just proved her mother was right and that Jane needed help?'

Other members agreed with this and felt that if he had persevered, the doctor might well have found that Jane was sectionable in the interests of her health. One carer was worried that the psychiatrist couldn't take being shouted at and threatened; this made no sense at all to her. 'It makes one wonder how a professional trained to work with serious mental illness could be so sensitive', she added.

Dropping out of the system

Members felt it was sad that her parents were still unable to get help for Jane after she had lost her job and partner; it seemed that even with these further indications that things were not right for her, the young woman was left to deteriorate further. She had to all intents and purposes dropped out of the system.

THE WIDER PERSPECTIVE

The group felt that the most important issue to come out of this sad case study was something they had noticed in previous cases. It seemed that professionals working with serious mental illness did not seem to realize the implication of a sufferer coming off medication and because of this there seemed to be no recognized plan of action to do something about this and immediately nip it in the bud.

One member, a carer, had been concerned when discussing Kay's experiences in the last chapter that professionals had not got together to find some way to do something about her stated intention to come off her medication. 'One thing which seems to be missing', he commented, 'is recognition of the likely course of a psychotic illness especially when medication is stopped'. He felt this was very apparent in Jane's case. The CPN team had explained to the mother that 'as Jane had moved and was doing so well in her job, this had seemed a good time to acknowledge that she didn't need specialist help any longer' and yet this decision appeared to have been made immediately after one of the team had tried in vain to persuade Jane to resume taking her medication. He wondered, therefore, if this was some sort of automatic reaction – to deter sufferers from coming off their medication – rather than any realization as to just how often the act of coming off medication heralded an imminent relapse?

This carer felt that if there was any real understanding about this subject, then professionals would make a much more immediate and concentrated effort to persuade a sufferer to stay on medication. Other members agreed with this and one, a survivor, reiterated her earlier comment that patients coming off medication need to be followed up thoroughly and for as long as it takes to ensure they are not in danger of relapsing. 'Any such follow up in Jane's case', she added, 'would have quickly demonstrated that her symptoms were returning. Action at that point might have prevented her losing her job and her partner, let alone suffering further damage to her health'.

Recognizing signs of relapse

The other point which particularly concerned the group was that a succession of warning signs were not acknowledged by anyone other than Jane's parents. As members have just pointed out, her coming off medication should have set alarm bells ringing, but when the mother talked to the GP about Jane's obscure physical symptoms returning, he could not see that this might be a repetition of his patient's experiences before she was prescribed anti-psychotic medication. Members felt it was a pity that he, and others, did not listen to the mother because it was natural that she would be likely to be the first to recognize abnormality in her daughter. They were right about this and research has demonstrated that close relatives can detect signs of relapse in sufferers before others do (3).

A survivor pointed out that ideally, following a first episode of psychosis, details should be recorded of any unusual signs, behaviour and stresses which were evident in the individual leading up to the breakdown. She felt this should always be done so that when those close to the sufferer see these signs again, they will be acknowledged as significant and acted upon. This was not just wishful thinking, she pointed out, as research has been carried out which demonstrates that professionals and families can work together in this way and take preventive action rather than awaiting a crisis situation (4).

Other members of the group agreed that anything at all which could be done to prevent, rather than wait for, a psychotic crisis had to be worthwhile and that, sadly, Jane's case proved this beyond any doubt.

Ongoing monitoring and care

Finally, members felt very strongly that a great deal of personal suffering and public money could be saved if potentially well individuals with an underlying serious mental illness remained in the system so that they could receive support if and when they needed this.

As one carer put it, referring back to an earlier comment, 'vulnerabilities will always remain and, like has been suggested, a body of knowledge should be built up about each individual so that everyone is aware of what might precipitate a relapse'. That way, she believed, these usually well sufferers and their relatives could rely on a quick response when this is needed. Other members agreed that this would ensure that most of these able sufferers could get on with their lives without having to face the ever present risk of further damage.

Equally, the group felt that a quick and effective response would also protect many of those sufferers who presently stumble from one crisis to another – 'part of the revolving door syndrome', as someone put it – or, worse, slip into a chronic illness after one relapse too many. Either way, members pointed out, nobody wins!

SUMMING UP

The general feeling in the group was that several important issues were raised in this case study. These included their observation that there seems to be a marked tendency among some professionals (a) to minimize the seriousness of a psychotic illness in individuals who appear to be bright and undamaged and (b) to under-rate the importance of medication in acute psychotic illness.

Most of all, members were concerned about the family's wasted efforts to obtain an effective response from the system. They were exasperated by the thwarted attempts of Jane's parents to get help for their daughter and wanted to know how these potentially well sufferers can get back into the system if no-one listens to those closest to them?

INFORMATION

The following pieces of information are relevant to points brought up during the group's analysis and discussion which have been highlighted in the text:

(1)   Effects of drug abuse on serious mental illness

Although little is yet understood about this, taking cannabis and similar drugs may be a trigger factor in the start of a psychotic illness; they certainly seem to feature sometimes in the prelude to a first episode, perhaps in an individual with a predisposition to this type of illness.

What is more clear, however, is that persevering with a habit of smoking cannabis can make a psychosis very difficult, if not impossible, to treat effectively.

(2)   Sufferers presenting physical problems to their GP

The following comment appeared in the *British Medical Journal* on 9th October 1993:

'Patients with schizophrenia consult (their GP) more often with physical complaints than the average patient, which may divert doctors from reviewing important mental health issues' (quoted in SANE's magazine *SANETALK*. Winter 1993).

(3)   The role of relatives in recognizing the early warning signs of relapse in a sufferer

Work carried out by psychologists at All Saints Hospital in Birmingham demonstrated that 59 per cent of relatives recognized the early warning signs a month before the relapse of a sufferer and 75 per cent recognized them at least two weeks before relapse. (Max Birchwood, Jo Smith *et al.* 'Predicting relapse in schizophrenia: the development and implementation of an early signs monitoring system using patients and families as observers, a preliminary investigation', *Psychological Medicine* (1989), 19, 649–656)

(4)   Professionals and families working in partnership to prevent further relapse

Successful work of this nature carried out by the above team of psychologists has been described by Jo Smith and Max Birchwood, 'Relatives and Patients as Partners in the Management of Schizophrenia: The Development of a Service Model, *British Journal of Psychiatry* (1990),156,654–660.

EXERCISE

Many sufferers with an acute psychotic illness can keep well and resume a normal lifestyle, having no need of the mental health services much of the time. Others like Jane slip out of the system before they are properly recovered.

These potentially well individuals can often stay well if they can receive help (usually in the form of a resumption or adjustment of medication) before the psychosis sets in.

How would you go about providing an appropriate response – ie, 'safety net' – for this potentially well population, bearing in mind you could use some of the money saved by avoiding costly crisis intervention.

CHAPTER 8

Getting appropriate treatment and care
A lottery?

Sometimes it does seem that there is a large element of chance as to whether or not a first-time episode of a serious mental illness will be recognized and acknowledged in time to prevent unnecessary damage and suffering. Similarly, once in the system, it seems to be something of a lottery whether or not the sufferer will slip through the net later. Let's take a look at five brief case studies before considering this further.

CASE STUDY

Andrew: Not long after his twentieth birthday, and after being involved in a serious road accident in which he suffered concussion, Andrew walked out on an excellent job, telling his mother that he knew he would die if he stayed there. A usually sensible and independent young man, he offered no further explanation and declined to discuss the matter. His parents were upset as well as amazed; they couldn't make any sense at all of his explanation and they knew how hard their youngest child had worked to obtain the position he had now turned his back on.

After he had been 'kicking his heels' for several weeks, his parents were quite relieved when Andrew announced that he was going to join an old school friend who was helping out on a farm in a neighbouring county. He kept this up for a couple of months and then moved on to a commune further south. A few weeks later he was home again, markedly changed. He was excitable and argumentative with his parents, up and about all night, playing noisy music with morbid words. Life became very difficult for the rest of the family and his mother was at a loss to know what to do. When Andrew talked enthusiastically about the commune one day, she agreed that it might be a good idea for him to go back there for a while, hoping he would sort himself out.

Five days later, a police officer rang to say that Andrew was at a police station ninety miles away asking for help to get home as a group of men were after him with guns. The police thought the young man was on drugs because he was acting so strangely and was glassy-eyed. They were wrong; it turned out that Andrew had neither eaten nor slept since he had left home. He was almost mute and was shaking with terror when his parents called for him at the police station.

Once home, Andrew followed his mother around, not letting her out of his sight. She contacted the family's GP, who came out as soon as his surgery had finished. By now, Andrew was mute and virtually motionless. After listening to the mother and trying to communicate with her son, the doctor left, saying this was schizophrenia and that Andrew would need to go to hospital. He then went away to organize things.

An approved social worker (ASW), came round and abruptly told Andrew he would have to go into the local mental hospital, so he fled the house. As she left, the ASW cheerfully assured his distraught mother that she need not worry; her son would be back! Andrew did eventually return, in a terrible state, very much later that night. A second ASW succeeded in arranging the admission to hospital without further delay.

The diagnosis given by the GP was later confirmed and Andrew remained in hospital for some months but later was re-admitted to hospital and has spent most of his time there over the past eleven years. He continues to have all the bizarre symptoms of an acute psychosis rather than showing any signs of slipping into a chronic schizophrenic illness. Unfortunately, he is hyper-sensitive to all the available drugs, having distressing side effects with most of them. They seem powerless to have much effect on the punishing delusions and severe paranoia which govern most of his actions, however mundane.

CASE STUDY

Naomi: With no previous history of mental problems, and two years into an ideally happy marriage, this 32-year-old woman suddenly started to fret about her job, becoming quite weepy about going in to work. When the situation did not improve, her GP put Naomi on sick leave and later he referred her to a psychiatrist who prescribed anti-depressants.

Three months later, Naomi showed no signs of being depressed and, indeed, was increasingly busy with all sorts of fund-raising activities and projects both at home and at church, successfully recruiting volunteers to help her raise monies for various 'special causes'. Her husband was becoming uneasy as his wife seemed tireless and confident in pursuing these activities while refusing to discuss returning to work. Similarly, although she was usually careful with money, she was spending quite a lot of the household budget on raising money for others, and was showing a distressing new tendency to find fault with him, becoming increasingly impatient and tetchy.

Naomi's excited activities reached a crescendo after she had gone three nights without sleep, at which point she explained to her exhausted husband that she would be particularly busy for a while as she now knew she was Jesus Christ returned to earth 'to put the world to rights', and she must urgently recruit her disciples. Her husband's anxious call to their GP was rewarded by an early home visit. The doctor took note of the fact that Naomi happened to have an out-patient appointment with her psychiatrist that morning. Meanwhile, her husband, having damaged his leg by slipping on the stairs during all the excitement of the previous night, sought his brother's help as Naomi had made it clear that it would be a waste of her precious time to go to the hospital for her appointment. He knew he would need some support in getting her there!

In the event, the psychiatrist seemed unsure what to do when her patient made it clear she had no intention of staying in hospital, and asked Naomi to come back and see her after lunch. Her husband and brother–in–law then spent a desperate two hours trying to keep Naomi from dashing off for a train for 'some business I have to do in London'. At the second appointment, the psychiatrist's assessment that Naomi needed to be in hospital was confirmed. As soon as she learned this, Naomi stormed out of the room and was half–way to the railway station when her brother–in–law caught up with her. He was more than a little surprised that no–one else had attempted to stop her leaving but eventually 'talked' his sister–in–law back to the hospital where she was admitted on a 72–hour section.

Naomi was quickly diagnosed as suffering with MD but neither this information, nor explanations of any sort were shared with the patient or her husband, although he kept asking for these. This, together with the sort of lax attitude on the ward that allowed for her to go off to a pub in the evenings with other patients, to drink as she pleased and to walk out into a busy street with no awareness of danger, led to the couple seeking a 'second' opinion and to Naomi's move to a private hospital.

Although she spent much of the time at home, she nevertheless remained very ill for around twelve months before making an excellent recovery with the help of maintenance medication, which she continues to take eight years later. Meanwhile, Naomi believes she would not have survived, let alone made such a excellent recovery, if she had stayed in the first hospital.

CASE STUDY

Joan: Middle–aged and a grandmother, this woman had no mental health problems until she reached her menopause. Suddenly, her mood changed over a few days and she became increasingly agitated, convinced that something terrible was about to happen to one of her family. It was as though a switch were turned on and everything had turned sinister and frightening. Not surprisingly, she became weepy and confused, despite the fact that her husband did everything he could to reassure her.

After two nights of sleeplessness and a growing conviction that she had been picked out for some terrible vengeance, Joan started to have bizarre and terrifying experiences which included hearing the neighbours saying she had to die and becoming aware that a stream of white cars were passing to and fro outside the house with the drivers watching her, to make sure she made no attempt to leave the house.

Her husband was so worried by his wife's behaviour, and, worse, by her evident stark terror, that he phoned the GP surgery that weekend. One of the senior doctors came round to the house to see his patient of many years. He asked all the questions which he believed might confirm his suspicions and he eventually told Joan and her husband that she was almost certainly suffering with a schizophrenic breakdown.

As Joan begged the doctor to let her stay at home, he gave her a trial dose injection of anti-psychotic medication there and then and arranged for a domiciliary visit by a psychiatrist. This specialist said they could not be certain at this stage about such a diagnosis, and clearly did not approve of schizophrenia having been mentioned, but nevertheless he arranged for the patient to continue to have a low-dose injection and some oral medication. He also arranged for a CPN to visit Joan regularly until things started to improve for her.

Joan made a very gradual recovery with continued CPN support and some sessions at a day-centre where she attended several groups. About ten months later she pleaded to come off the medication. Although this was done gradually, Joan quickly begun relapsing into a psychosis once more, finally confirming the GP's original diagnosis. When she was stabilized on the same dose of medication that she had taken for most of the time she had been recovering from her breakdown, Joan began to make real progress again.

Although she had no trouble coming to terms with her medical condition, and in fact took an active interest in learning everything she could about it, it was a long time before Joan could settle for the need to take medication indefinitely. As she explained, she didn't have side effects from the drugs, it was just the principle of the thing; needing to take drugs permanently when she had had no mental health problems of any sort until she was a grandmother! Joan put herself at risk twice more by cutting back on the dose

Joan put herself at risk twice more by cutting back on the dose before she finally accepted what had happened and resumed taking an effective amount of the medication and set about getting on with the rest of her life.

CASE STUDY

Ron: On leaving school, Ron was unable to find work. Previously happy–go–lucky, he became increasingly moody. He started to spend a lot of his time in his room, with the curtains drawn, playing his favourite tapes and CDs at full volume. He avoided his family and his old friends and, apart from frequent visits to his doctor's surgery, he rarely went out of the house. When Ron's parents sought the help of the GP, she agreed to have a closer look at him the next time he came to the surgery. It seemed that he kept coming to see her, with a continuous list of physical ailments, all of which came to nothing.

When the GP later tackled Ron about how he was really feeling, his behaviour became so defensive and bizarre that she asked a psychiatrist to visit him in his home. The specialist suggested the young man might be having a 'mild psychotic episode' and prescribed tablets for him to take, asking Ron's brother to go out and fetch the prescription so that the doctor could encourage his patient to take some medication. Before leaving the house, the psychiatrist told Ron that he wanted to see him at his out–patient's clinic and asked his parents to make sure that he continued to take the medication. This they did and were relieved to find their son quickly becoming his old self again, even obtaining part–time work at a local cafe. Meanwhile, Ron's father went along to the first out–patient appointment, but after that his son insisted on going on his own.

Before long, the family became aware that Ron was starting to avoid them again and soon realized that things were no better than when they first sought help for him. In fact they were worse because their son now refused to have anything to do with the GP. When they turned to her for help again, the doctor explained to the parents that she could not force her attentions on him. And that, it seemed, was that.

Fifteen months after the GP first intervened, Ron went to the cafe where he had briefly worked and threatened the owner with a kitchen knife. She managed to calm him down and called the police. Ron was admitted to hospital under section and was stabilized on depot injections before he was discharged three months later. For the first time, his parents learned that Ron had a schizophrenic illness, and what this meant. They also discovered that their son had not kept any of his outpatient appointments after the first one and that he had stockpiled dozens of tablets – which he had previously pretended to swallow – in the corner of a bedroom drawer.

Ron has had two further relapses in four years. He has not been able to take up work again and appears to have now slipped into a chronic illness. He sits around all day if his mother gets him out of bed and complains that he has no energy and that everything is flat and grey. His parents are hurt and bewildered that Ron takes no interest in anything that happens in the home and avoids other members of the family, absenting himself from any 'get-togethers' or other special events in their lives. They cannot believe this is the cheerful and outgoing boy they used to know.

CASE STUDY

Karen: Her parents first noticed changes in her behaviour when Karen was thirteen-years-old. She started to lock herself in her room rather than join her family in the lounge. At times she would listen to loud music or watch television till very late at night. At other times, she was uninterested in everything and seemed to make heavy weather of her school work. When she did socialize with the family, there were frequent unprovoked outbursts and rows. Her younger sister, eleven years old at the time, found these particularly upsetting.

Their mother was a teacher and worried that she was being too analytical about the situation. Perhaps this was normal adolescence they were seeing in Karen? However, after six months, she and her husband mentioned the problems they were having to their GP and eventually persuaded Karen to visit him. The doctor suggested some form of 'family therapy' might be helpful and, after some considerable delay, this was eventually arranged, on a six-weekly basis, in a town forty miles away.

All four of the family had to attend and, as appointments were on weekdays, the parents had to take a day off work and both daughters lost school time. Suggestions and advice from the child psychiatrist and his team focused mainly on the perceived failings of the parents. The mother, it seemed, was too oppressive and demanding and the father was said to be weak. At this point, it seemed to both parents that things were fast reaching an all-time low. Each had come to the sessions, as parents do, convinced in their own minds that it must be their fault that their child was having all these problems but now their very personalities and characters were being called into question and found to be lacking. Exhausted from sleepless nights and the increasing turmoil at home, they were now tempted to look at each other and their marriage critically. Meanwhile, their younger child was suffering from these new tensions in the family as well as from her sister's unpredictable and upsetting behaviour.

Perhaps it was as well that these parents were as sensible as they were caring and they recognized that neither child was gaining from the family therapy which was even starting to threaten their own marriage. They eventually talked this through with each other and resolved not to allow potentially destructive messages from third parties to wreak further havoc on the family. Instead, they resolved to apply themselves to finding out what had happened to their elder child, and what helped her and what didn't.

As a result of extensive reading around the subject, the mother begun to suspect that Karen's problems might stem from a manic depressive illness. She discussed this at length with her husband and they returned to their GP some four years after they had first sought his help, putting their case to him. The doctor was happy to refer Karen to the adult mental health services at this point and before long the tentative diagnosis was confirmed; Karen had MD. She was prescribed lithium and seemed happy enough to take this regularly. Her parents shared their hard-earned knowledge about the illness with their daughters to help them come to terms with what had happened. They were amply rewarded for their efforts by watching the family settle down during the next few months and Karen gradually resume a normal lifestyle.

Because of her experiences, Karen decided that she would like to work in a caring profession. She was also determined to go about achieving this without hiding her mental health history. Although her local general hospital turned down her application to become a nurse, Karen was accepted for training at a famous teaching hospital.

Six years on, Karen is married with two young daughters. After the second child was born, she gradually came off her lithium and there has been no sign of her old symptoms returning.

COMMENT

When LEAP Group members came to analyse and discuss these five cases, they found several factors cropping up which they had identified in earlier chapters as having a significant influence on a new sufferer's chances of getting safely into the system.

Before going on to read the rest of this chapter, it might be worthwhile to pause for a moment and look through these short case studies once more with this in mind. After doing this, you might like to make a note of any factors which (a) might make it more likely that a new sufferer's illness will be recognized and treated appropriately and (b) might make it more likely that he or she will then stay safely in the system.

GROUP'S ANALYSIS OF THESE CASE STUDIES

Members felt that three of these five cases were not really typical of most of those they come across, in that the sufferers concerned seemed to get into the system very quickly indeed. It seemed that this was due to the pro-active approach of their GPs.

The role of the GP in obtaining a quick diagnosis

Members noted that Naomi's GP quickly referred his patient to a psychiatrist and that Andrew's and Joan's GPs immediately referred their patients to the mental health services and also had no hesitation in diagnosing schizophrenia on the spot. Interestingly, no-one in the group found fault with this; as one carer remarked, 'far better an early diagnosis than one that's too late!'

A survivor pointed out that the criteria now used by most psychiatrists for diagnosing schizophrenia (1) do not allow for such a prompt acknowledgement because these state that the symptoms must be present for six months before such a diagnosis can be made. Members wondered why this should be so; it seemed to them that the sooner the diagnosis was acknowledged, the more chance the sufferer had of obtaining effective treatment and appropriate after–care. This is an increasingly popular opinion and even back in 1977 two psychiatrists, very much respected as leading authorities in their generation, emphasized that early recognition and treatment of a schizophrenic illness is paramount (2). More recently, of course, research has confirmed this viewpoint (3).

The presenting of physical symptoms: a common phenomenon

Several members pointed out that it seemed that Ron's illness was missed for some time by his GP who did not question his frequent visits to her surgery with a succession of physical symptoms. A carer remarked that this was reminiscent of what happened to Jane, in Chapter 7, and to other cases she had heard about. It seemed to her that those sufferers 'who present themselves in a coherent way and complain only of physical symptoms seem less likely to receive the help they need'. It is noteworthy that this phenomenon was brought to the attention of doctors in the British Medical Journal three years before the present discussion took place (4).

Falling by the wayside

Members noted that Ron was nevertheless eminently treatable when his GP referred him for psychiatric help as he immediately responded to the medication. They were amazed that while the psychiatrist apparently understood that there could be problems with getting his patient to take medication, arranging for the first dose to be taken before he left the house, he then left it at that. 'Surely', a survivor wanted to know, 'he didn't believe that solved the problem once and for all?'

This matter intrigued group members and, after some further discussion, a carer said 'it seems that professionals sometimes do not realize that the nature of a psychotic illness means that the sufferer is unlikely to be able to *self-manage* – to take medication and keep appointments – until the illness is well stabilized'.

Members felt that this psychiatrist compounded the problem by expecting the parents to make sure the medication was taken, without first giving them the benefit of any explanations about this type of illness, let alone about the reasons for taking the drugs! Indeed, as one carer pointed out, 'Ron's parents didn't know that their son could deceive them by keeping the tablets under his tongue and removing them later – why should they? – but tens of thousands of carers could have told them this' and, a survivor agreed, 'unless he was totally ignorant about psychotic behaviour, so could the psychiatrist.'

A carer, who had expressed misgivings over the follow-up of out-patients in an earlier chapter, pointed out that 'again, we see in the case of Ron, that he did not turn up for appointments with the psychiatrist and nobody followed this up. Why didn't they?' Members agreed that this should be a mandatory part of after-care; as one of them had pointed out in an earlier chapter, 'missed appointments are bad news in a serious mental illness'. Finally, members were disturbed to note that the GP refused the parents' request for help when Ron was becoming ill again, using the same reason that the GP in Malcolm's case (see Chapter 5) gave in similar circumstances, that she couldn't force her attentions on him. A survivor pointed out that this was a golden opportunity to bring the psychiatrist back into the picture and other members agreed. They couldn't understand why some GPs fail to 'stop the rot' at this point. As one carer commented, 'when you are desperate and you get this sort of response – that is when you begin to believe the rest of the world has gone mad!'

Yet another very young sufferer

Members noticed with concern that Karen and her family had the same sort of experiences as Malcolm in Chapter 5 and Kay in Chapter 6. In each case the parents were judged and found wanting; their problems were seen to stem from their assumed failings rather than from a mental illness in their child. It seemed to the group that this sort of reasoning could only apply if those carrying out the assessments were either ignorant about serious mental illness or unaware that it can strike young people in their early teens. The group were again dismayed by a lack of evidence of sensitivity and caring in those who could, at least, have helped these families cope with their prolonged pain.

Members took the view that this particular family survived in spite of the service they received rather than because of it. As one asked, 'what would have happened to Karen if her mother had not been so resourceful?'

Summing up – five case studies

Andrew: The group felt that Andrew's case was dealt with promptly and that it was unfortunate that no medication has helped him up to now. The general feeling was that Andrew's illness could have been caused by his accident and that this was probably the reason why it was proving so difficult to treat.

Naomi: Members were delighted for Naomi that the outcome of her illness was so successful. They were nonetheless concerned that the level of care and protection at the first hospital was such that she feels she would not have survived the worst part of her illness if she had stayed there.

Joan: It seemed to members that Joan's case seemed to be an excellent example of how a new sufferer can be treated and cared for outside of hospital. The outstanding features of this case, they felt, was the prompt diagnosis and prescription of appropriate treatment, from 'a GP who knew his patient well', and the provision of ongoing and effective after-care.

Ron: The group have discussed Ron's case in some detail in their analysis above and the general feeling was that he had been very unfortunate and had received a wholly unsatisfactory service. Ron was in fact lost to the system even as his psychosis was acknowledged.

Karen: The group was delighted about the outcome of Karen's story, but felt this could have ended very differently if it hadn't been for the strength and determined efforts of the parents. They were particularly heartened by the young woman's successful efforts to get on with her chosen career without needing to hide her diagnosis.

THE WIDER PERSPECTIVE

It seemed to members that some new sufferers are far more fortunate than others in the response they receive from the mental health services. They felt this could not be an acceptable state of affairs. As one carer pointed out, 'we are talking about what happens to desperately vulnerable people when they need help. With serious mental illness, you often don't get a second chance if that help comes too late'. On this sobering note, the group decided to take a closer look at which factors seem to influence whether or not sufferers obtain the help and protection they need.

Prompt recognition of a serious mental illness

Members felt that cases already known to them, as well as those studied in the present and previous chapters of this book, demonstrated that psychotic illness was just like any other illness; the sooner it is treated the better.[2][3] Where psychotic symptoms are left untreated for long periods, albeit a first episode of illness or a relapse, then there is clearly a real risk of further deterioration and also of slipping into a chronic illness.

Young sufferers – at special risk of delays?

They found that younger sufferers – Malcolm, Kay, Karen and others mentioned by members in Chapter 5 – seemed to wait indefinitely for recognition of their illness. In all but one of these cases they waited for a diagnosis until they were of an age to be referred to the adult mental health service.

Members felt that a survivor summed up the general feeling among them when they were discussing Kay's case in Chapter 6, with 'there should be a straightforward psychiatric assessment made of any young person in this situation. If it doesn't come to anything, it doesn't matter, but then at least it has been checked out'. This certainly seemed to be a factor which was lacking in all of these cases and members felt that this was an unacceptable omission.

A lack of explanations

The group felt that after a prompt diagnosis and appropriate treatment, the next most important factor in a good recovery was to make sure that the family, and the sufferer when the time was right, should receive adequate explanations about the illness and the implications of this. They felt it to be a cause for concern that these explanations were significantly lacking in the cases discussed in this book and that this reflected their own experiences and those of other families they knew. This lack of information, in the group's opinion, made sufferers more vulnerable to relapse than any other factor.

Against overwhelming odds

Members felt that leaving families to look after a new sufferer without adequate explanations was particularly reprehensible when the illness had not first been stabilized with the appropriate treatment. The psychiatrists who diagnosed both Barry in Chapter 4 and Ron in this chapter not only neglected to arrange for them to be immediately monitored and stabilized on medication in hospital, they also neglected to ensure that the parents had a proper understanding of the mammoth task of trying to do this at home on their own.

Staying in the system

Once safely into the system, members felt that it was those who seemed to have the most to lose who were particularly vulnerable to slipping out of it again; that is, those sufferers who make a good recovery and show little, if any, signs of damage. It did seem that professionals were more likely to see them as having no further need of the services, as in Jane's case, or even doubt the original diagnosis, as in Marie's case. As one member put it, 'these sufferers can be lost to the system simply because they are seen as being well enough to no longer be in need of help and support.' This survivor felt that such an assumption should never be made; she knew sufferers holding down very responsible jobs who continue indefinitely to receive support and monitoring, regardless of how well they are doing and regardless of whether or not they are still on maintenance medication. The group felt that this had to be a caring and sensible practice in that it enabled these individuals properly to fulfil their potential. Both they and society gained – at minimal cost to the system.

The need for a co-ordinated service

In fact, everyone agreed that provision of careful monitoring and follow-up, or, at the very least and where this is adequate for that individual, a life-line, should be mandatory for everyone with a serious mental illness. This, it seemed to the group, could only be achieved within a co-ordinated service. However, it sometimes seemed that the present system was made up of various agencies and individuals – some much more caring and conscientious than others – all seemingly working within a vacuum, with little communication with each other and even less with the families taking the brunt of community care. LEAP group felt this explained much of the present variations in service received by individuals with a serious mental illness.

SUMMING UP

In this chapter, the group looked at five case studies and although three of these cases have turned out encouragingly well, members found evidence to suggest that getting safely into the system does seem to be something of a lottery and that even those who make good recoveries sometimes make them in spite of, rather than because of, the service they receive. In particular, they felt that professionals failed to share information about serious mental illness with the very individuals who had to get on and live with this, ie, sufferers and their families.

In these case studies, as in others discussed in this book, members found encouraging evidence of good practice and real caring as well as disturbing evidence of neither! They found that the quality of the services which sufferers received varied quite alarmingly; so much so that this disparity could explain why some individuals become so very ill and dependent on hard pressed services.

INFORMATION

The following pieces of information are relevant to points brought up during the group's analysis and discussion which have been highlighted in the text:

(1)   Criteria for diagnosing schizophrenia

A recognized and accepted set of criteria for diagnosing this illness, as laid out in the *Diagnostic and Statistical Manual of Mental Disorders*, 4th edition (known as DSMIV and published by the American Psychiatric Association), include a stipulation that the symptoms must have been present for six months or more. This sort of arbitrary measurement undoubtedly helps to standardize diagnostic practice and facilitate research but it is less helpful in protecting the interests of individual sufferers in need of immediate treatment and care. Many sufferers realize when well again that they were having symptoms long before they were aware of this and long before there were any outwards signs of illness. Who, in these circumstances, can judge at *the time when it matters* how long symptoms have been present? And does it matter, when some immediately recognizable cases seemingly 'come out of the blue' and erupt overnight, demanding immediate treatment and care?

(2)   A need for immediate acknowledgement of a schizophrenic illness?

Two leading psychiatrists of their time have commented:
'When treatment was restricted to institutional care and occupation therapy, early diagnosis was scarcely important, but with the coming of the modern physical treatments and the realization that the best results are obtained in early cases, it has become of the first importance to recognize the illness at its beginnings.'
(Slater, E. and Roth, M. (1977) *Clinical Psychiatry*, 3rd edition. London: Baillière Tindall, p.308.)

(3)   The dangers of delays in obtaining appropriate treatment

(a)   A large extended study of first episodes of schizophrenia revealed that the most important determinant of relapse was duration of illness prior to starting neuroleptic medication. (Crow, T.J. *et al.* (1986) The Northwick Park Study of First Episodes of Schizophrenia, Part II, 'A randomized controlled trial of prophylactic neuroleptic treatment', *British Journal of Psychiatry148*, pp.120–7.)

(b)   Richard Jed Wyatt has concluded, in his comprehensive overview of the use of neuroleptic medication and the natural course of schizophrenia, that 'some patients are left with a damaging residual if a psychosis is allowed to proceed unmitigated.

While psychosis is undoubtedly demoralizing and stigmatizing, it may also be biologically toxic'. (Wyatt, R.J. (1991) 'Neuroleptics and the natural course of schizophrenia.' *Schizophrenia Bulletin 17*, 2).

(4)   Sufferers presenting physical problems to their GP

The following comment appeared in the *British Medical Journal* on 9th October 1993,

'Patients with schizophrenia consult (their GP) more often with physical complaints than the average patient, which may divert doctors from reviewing important mental health issues (quoted in SANE's magazine *SANETALK*, Winter 1993).'

EXERCISE

Undoubtedly the obtaining of appropriate treatment and care for a serious mental illness can become something of a lottery. For example, factors such as the age of the sufferer at the time of a first episode and the level of skills and dedication of individual professionals can dramatically influence the outcome of this type of illness.

Imagine you have been commissioned to standardize the services provided in every case of serious mental illness. How would you set about trying to achieve this?

CHAPTER 9

Getting into the system
Summing up

In the previous chapters of this book, we have looked at the sort of problems which can occur in obtaining a diagnosis and treatment for a first episode of a serious mental illness. LEAP group has studied eleven case studies and attempted to determine which, if any, factors seem to deter new sufferers from 'getting into the system'. Similarly, the group also looked to see if there were any common factors which make it more likely that a sufferer will later slip through the net.

Let's take a further look at the group's findings. Rather than make continual reference to one chapter or another, I have used the names of individuals discussed earlier in the book and would remind readers that, if required, the relevant pages in the text can be found under 'Case Studies' in the Index.

UNHELPFUL FACTORS

LEAP group found the following factors tended to militate against a successful outcome of a first episode of a psychotic illness:

Delays in obtaining acknowledgement of a serious mental illness

As we noted in Chapter 1, delays in 'getting into the system' with a first episode of serious mental illness are legion and are well chronicled. At a more personal level, half of of the members of LEAP group suffered considerable delays before obtaining a diagnosis and treatment for themselves or a loved one. They remain concerned about such delays as it quite clear that untreated psychotic symptoms are bad news for sufferers and those closest to them.

Members felt that young teenage sufferers seemed particularly vulnerable to really prolonged delays. This applied to Malcolm, Kay and Karen and other young people known to the group and discussed in Chapter 5. One factor was common to all of these cases; they were all of an age to be referred to the child psychiatry service. Their serious mental illness was not recognized at the time of referral nor, it seems, at any time while they were supervised by this service. Generally, it seems that they were regarded as having behavioural problems which stemmed from faulty parenting. Later – in some cases much later – their serious mental illness was diagnosed and treated. Out of the three young individuals we discussed in detail, Karen's manic depressive illness has seemingly abated but Malcolm and Kay remain exceptionally vulnerable.

Delays caused by sufferer seeking help for physical symptoms only

When Jane was becoming psychotic, she turned up at her GP's surgery regularly with a succession of physical ailments. Although this was out of character for this young woman and the things she complained of were quite obscure, even bizarre, the GP did not suspect that his patient might be mentally ill even when all tests proved negative. More surprisingly, he did not accept that it was all happening again when Jane's mother later sought his help for her daughter.

These frequent visits to their GP's surgery was a feature of Ron's and, to a lesser extent, Malcolm's cases and in several others known to LEAP group and, as we have noted, this phenomenon has been commented on in the medical press.

Delays in learning one's diagnosis

Jackie and Marie were victims of this sort of delay. In fact, Jackie and her family never did find out about the diagnosis until her treatable acute condition had slipped into a chronic schizophrenic illness. They were given no explanations which could have helped her to stay well.

In Marie's case, she was convinced she was mad and that no-one could help her because she was the only one like this. As has been the case with most sufferers known to LEAP group, Marie started to make real progress once she learned about her illness.

'Self-management' for a first episode of psychosis?

Both Barry and Ron were provisionally assessed by psychiatrists making a domiciliary visit and both were prescribed anti-psychotic medication and given follow-up out-patient appointments. However, hospitalization at that time would have allowed for them to be properly assessed, monitored and, hopefully, stabilized on the appropriate medication but this was not arranged for either of these young men. The responsibility for their keeping well eventually fell on the sufferers themselves and their parents, although none of them had any of the information they needed to make a success of this. In effect, both these sufferers were doomed to slip through the net even as they were 'getting into the system'.

GPs and other professionals declining to intervene

The parents of both Malcolm and Ron returned to their GPs for help when their sons refused to attend outpatient appointments and had virtually dropped out of the system. Both doctors declined to intervene, explaining they couldn't force their attentions on a patient who was not seeking their help. This sort of situation, of course, calls for a domiciliary visit by a psychiatrist – a service available via the GP – or a mental health assessment. In both cases nothing was done until others were put at risk and the police had to intervene.

Similarly, when Jane's mental health was seriously deteriorating, a psychiatrist and community nurses turned away because the sufferer made it clear she didn't want their help. In the case of the doctor, he turned his back on his patient because she had shouted abuse at him and then reported him for calling at her house. She had to wait a further 18 months for the help she needed.

Professionals declining to use the law

LEAP group noted that in addition to these examples of professionals declining to intervene because the sufferer wasn't actively seeking their help, there were also instances where professionals working with the

Mental Health Act 1983 declined to use the law to protect a sufferer. Even when Malcolm threatened his mother with a knife in front of his young brothers, he was later admitted to hospital voluntarily, and then quite predictably discharged himself. When Kay had kept well for three years after being ill throughout her teens, professionals did not section her 'in the interests of her health' when she was clearly deteriorating. When Jane's life was collapsing around her, despite earlier calls for help by her mother, she floundered for 18 months before she at last obtained help, and this was eventually achieved by the use of the mental health legislation.

OTHER CAUSES FOR CONCERN

These, then, were factors which the LEAP group found cropping up in cases where sufferers have not fared well or, in a couple of cases, waited much longer for a good recovery than should have been necessary. Rather differently, there were other features in 'the system', of a more general nature, which also concerned members:

A disparity in quality of service

Members were startled at the variation in the quality of services which sufferers received; they felt this disparity could at least partly explain why some sufferers thrive and others fall by the wayside. In particular, the group felt that a sufferer's progress, or otherwise, was often influenced by the level of caring and persistence of individual professionals and that this could be seen to vary enormously.

A lack of communication and explanations

One feature which the group found which seems to be almost constant, and a part of a general failure in communication, is the lack of essential information reaching those having to cope with a serious mental illness; in other words, sufferers and their families. As we have noted some members of the LEAP group have personal experience of this system as being aware of many other families who have also been deprived of vital information. This often became available only when they met up with others 'who have been there'. Members feel that it is essential that all new sufferers and their families should be given the opportunity to get in touch with voluntary organizations such as the Manic Depression Fellowship (MDF), National Schizophrenia Fellowship (NSF) and SANE, which specialize in providing information on this sort of illness.

Finally, the group noted that this lack of explanations could even include not being told one's diagnosis. In particular, members were appalled to think that Jackie and her husband could be kept in ignorance of her diagnosis even though her doctors would be expected to pass that information on to third parties under certain circumstances.

The undervaluing of families

Members could not understand why families continue to be undervalued both as a source of information – for example, on the past history and on the day-to-day progress of a sufferer – and as a major provider of community care. LEAP group believes that individuals with a serious mental illness will fare much better when attitudes about the role of the family change and particularly when relatives don't have the sort of problem that Jane's mother had when she tried to persuade professionals that her daughter was becoming ill again.

Professional training and expertise

On discussing several of the cases in this book and bearing in mind other cases they know, LEAP group members were concerned about a lack of understanding in some professionals about psychosis and psychotic behaviour. It seemed to them that rivalry between the individual professions had led to the adoption of a variety of approaches to the handling of serious mental illness. The group felt that this in turn may well have contributed to an eroding of basic knowledge and expertise on the course and nature of conditions such as manic depression and schizophrenia.

A need for feedback?

Group members felt that one way to make up for any such erosion of knowledge and expertise would be for agencies to provide feedback for the professionals involved in each case of serious mental illness so that they can see for themselves what has helped and what hasn't. It seemed to them that a variety of theories and approaches, aggravated by a frequent lack of continuity in any one case, provides little opportunity for learning from experience and, perhaps, for job satisfaction.

An accolade

Finally, while LEAP group appreciates that there is increasing pressure on the under–resourced mental health services, members noted that this did not seem to deter the inspired efforts of some truly dedicated professionals.

The group felt that certain measures could be taken which would not only promote and encourage this standard of practice, but they would also minimize private suffering and public spending. These are as follows:

SOME RECOMMENDATIONS

(1) **The system should acknowledge that everyone has a right to know their own diagnosis** – even while this is still provisional – **and the implications of this**. Fears of labelling should not be allowed to deprive families of their right to vital information, and this should include an introduction to relevant voluntary organizations.

(2) **There should be pro–active screening for first episodes of psychotic illness in referrals too young for the adult mental health services.** When young sufferers endure prolonged delays before receiving appropriate treatment, they should be treated as especially vulnerable in order to protect them from further damage.

(3) **The system should acknowledge the continuing vulnerability of seemingly well sufferers.** It is the ones with excellent potential to be well who particularly depend on a quick response – usually a temporary adjustment of medication – at the first signs of relapse. This is often not possible if they have to get back into the system first and the delays incurred can lead to a breakdown and the risk of real damage.

(4) Certain baselines should be set for every referral, to include

- **a proper assessment,** and monitoring and stabilizing for all first–time episodes of serious mental illness

- **the recording of any signs and changes leading up to the illness,** so that professionals and families can be alerted to further threats of relapse

- **immediate follow–up of all failed appointments** and of any sufferers reducing or rejecting their medication

- **pro–active measures to protect sufferers at times when they are too ill to seek help for themselves**

CONCLUSION

In this chapter we have looked again at the factors that the LEAP group found cropping up in those cases in which sufferers were not served well by the system. We then went on to look at more general issues which concerned its members. Finally, we looked at the sort of recommendations which the group believes could minimize private suffering as well as public spending.

If we lived in a perfect world, it's possible that all these issues might be addressed but, as it is, LEAP group members will be well pleased if their observations provide food for thought for those who are in a position to ensure the best possible outcome for everyone who has to cope with a serious mental illness.

Glossary

The term serious (or severe) mental illness refers to those conditions which can cause sufferers to become psychotic, so losing touch with reality. The most common of these are schizophrenia and manic depression. The following brief, and inevitably over-simplified, definitions may help readers who are not well acquainted with these illnesses.

MANIC DEPRESSION (MD)

This illness is an 'affective' disorder with severe mood swings. The individual may at any one time experience profound depression or mania. Sufferers describe their depressive episodes as being enveloped by a dark cloud but many experience a manic episode as being exciting and euphoric; a brilliant and creative phase. That is, until their 'high' escalates out of control and they slip into a psychosis, at which point the euphoria can become a disaster, once more disrupting the sufferer's life.

Mania begins with a build-up of symptoms, including a general **speeding up of movement and speech; a lack of sleep; enhanced creativity and awareness; an inflated self-confidence,** alongside increasing **irritability and impatience with others.** There is often **pressure of speech** (a compulsive need to talk continuously); **flight of ideas** (an inability to follow through one line of thought or idea); **a disturbing loss of judgement** (putting the individual very much at risk); lots of grand ideas, including a **preoccupation with spending money** and a **lack of inhibition** which, in some cases, can lead to uncharacteristic **promiscuity.** At this stage of a manic episode, it is not uncommon for the sufferer to experience some of the psychotic symptoms listed under 'acute' schizophrenia below.

The depressive episodes in MD may be seen as the 'down' and reverse side of mania, and the sufferer's experience may include a general **slowing down of movement and speech; a lack of energy and motivation; increased inhibition; impaired concentration**

and ability to undertake the simplest tasks; distorted feelings of guilt and self-loathing; anxiety and agitation and morbid thoughts of death, and, worse, **suicidal ideas**. Severe depression can escalate into a psychosis with hallucinations and delusions, but this is not so common as with mania.

These days, the excesses of MD can usually be controlled by one of the various mood-stabilizing drugs now available and the prognosis can be good. However, some individuals suffer distressing side-effects and one of these can be a dampening down of their often considerable creative ability which may make them reluctant to comply with treatment.

SCHIZOPHRENIA

The 'acute' form of schizophrenia is characterized by a cluster of so-called 'positive' symptoms and these include (a) **hallucinations,** when any of, or all, five senses may play tricks on the individual, the most common being the 'hearing of voices', (b) **delusions,** when all sorts of incredible ideas become fixed beliefs in the individual's mind and impervious to any reasoned argument. The most distressing and damaging of these can be the **paranoia** which convinces sufferers that other people – usually those who matter most to them – are plotting against them, and (c) **thought disturbance** with sufferers having all sorts of bizarre experiences such as finding their thoughts have taken on a life of their own, leading to ideas that their minds have been taken over by an outside source. These then are examples of the sort of experiences we call 'positive' symptoms, which make up the main part of an 'acute' schizophrenic illness. They are usually controlled by anti-psychotic medication but some 'acute' sufferers relapse into further psychotic episodes, particularly if they cut down or discontinue their medication. Because of this, there is an urgent need for a preventive approach to the handling of this illness.

The *chronic* form of schizophrenia is characterized by an ongoing and persistent cluster of 'negative' symptoms (so called because they take something away from the individual's original personality) which are disabling and in many ways quite different to those of acute schizophrenia. These include severe **lethargy**; profound **apathy; poverty of speech**, precluding any real ability to initiate conversation or indulge in what we know as 'small talk', **impaired concentration** making it difficult to even read a few lines of a newspaper; **emotional blunting**, in which sufferers may demonstrate no interest in or emotions about those closest to them and a general flatness in a 'grey' world where they feel no anticipation or excitement, with none of the highs and lows most of us experience in everyday life. All this can be socially crippling and amount to severe impairment and a change in personality which can make sufferers, and those closest to them, feel they have lost the person they once knew.

Despite the differences in the 'acute' and 'chronic' forms of the illness, there is an overlap between them. 'Acute' sufferers can experience some of these 'negative' symptoms following a breakdown and, tragically, some slip into the chronic form of the illness after one breakdown too many. Similarly, many 'chronic' sufferers can relapse into acute episodes of the illness, particularly if they are not protected by 'maintenance' medication.

General Glossary

Approved Social Worker (ASW): a professional, without medical training, who is qualified to work with the mental health law and to determine whether or not to make application for a sufferer's compulsory admission to hospital (given the required medical recommendations are available).

Community Psychiatric Nurse (CPN): a professional who provides ongoing support and care for the patient in the community. Also monitors medication and gives injections.

Delusion: a firmly held belief which has no basis in reality.

Family Theories: popular theories from the 1960s and 1970s, now discredited, which blamed families for their relative's schizophrenic illness.

Depot Injection: an injection into the muscle tissue of neuroleptic medication which is then slowly released, lasting anything from one to four weeks.

Genetic Risk: while we all have a 1 per cent chance of becoming schizophrenic at some time during our lives, research points to a raised risk in individuals with relatives who are sufferers; with one parent or brother or sister – 10 per cent; with two parents – 30 per cent; with an identical twin – 45 per cent.

GP: a doctor providing general medical treatment and care within the community who is the 'gateway' to all psychiatric services. Can also recommend their patient's compulsory admission to hospital.

Hallucination: an altered or abnormal perception affecting one's hearing, vision, taste, smell or touch. The most common type is auditory – the hearing of 'voices' for which there is no rational explanation.

Labelling Theory: popular theory originating from the 1960s claiming that a diagnosis of mental illness is little more than a stigmatized label put on someone who is 'deviant'. Consequently, professionals (rather than sufferers and their families) still tend to avoid acknowledging psychotic illness.

Mental Health Assessment: an assessment by an ASW and doctor(s) to determine whether or not someone mentally ill needs to be compulsorily admitted to hospital.

Nearest Relative: defined by the law and often the elder of a sufferer's parents or the spouse. Has certain rights, including that of making application for the individual's compulsory admission to hospital (given the required medical recommendations are available) if an ASW declines to do this.

Neuroleptic Medication: the drugs which have been used since the early 1950s to control psychotic symptoms. New ones have become available during the 1990s, helping some of those unaffected by the original medication.

Occupational Therapist: a professional who works with individual or groups of patients in hospital or in the community, facilitating rehabilitation and supporting them in adapting to an appropriate lifestyle.

Paranoia: a common and distressing delusion in a psychotic illness, with sufferers believing that others – usually those who most matter to them – have turned against them.

Personality Disorder: a little understood blanket term and an unwelcome label received by many individuals with a serious mental illness before their psychotic behaviour is properly understood and diagnosed.

Police: often involved in crisis work; can use Section 136 of the Mental Health Act, 1983, to take someone from a public area to a 'safe place' such as hospital or police station if they appear to be seriously mentally ill, so that an ASW can arrange a mental health assessment.

Psychiatrist: a doctor in charge of patients' psychiatric treatment in hospital and in the community. Can also recommend their compulsory admission to hospital.

Psychiatric Nurse: a professional who can work within a hospital, a formal hostel or the community, providing nursing care and support and the monitoring/administration of medication. See also CPN.

Psychosis: a condition in which sufferers lose touch with reality and have no recognition of the fact that they are mentally ill and in need of help. When this happens it usually means that treatment cannot be administered unless professionals use the mental health law to admit the individual to hospital.

Sectioning: the use of the law to compulsorily admit someone with a mental illness to hospital.

Serious Mental Illness: conditions such as manic depression and schizophrenia which can cause the individual to lose touch with reality, ie, to become psychotic.

Social Worker: a professional concerned with arranging accommodation for patients and assessing, as appropriate, other practical needs. May provide support for sufferers in the community and/or their families, usually on a short-term basis. See also ASW.

Further reading

Department of Health and Welsh Office (1993) *CODE OF PRACTICE: Mental Health Act 1983*: HMSO. Available from HMSO, PO Box 276, London SW8 5DT (tel 0171–873 9090).
This edition of the Code of Practice should really be mandatory reading for all professionals who work with the seriously mentally ill or, at the very least, be made readily available for reference purposes at the work place. Also useful for families caught up in a crisis situation which may call for resort to the law.

Copeland, M.E. (1994) *Living with Depression and Manic Depression.* Harbinger Publications Incorporated.
Beautifully presented and useful book from the USA by an MD sufferer and campaigner. She outlines a day-by-day self-management approach to coping with this type of illness (which could perhaps best be described as 'working in partnership' with professionals and a selected group of supporters). Includes advice on drawing up advance directives, or 'living wills', and generally brings a new meaning to the words 'self-determination'.

Greer, C. and Wing, J. (1988) *Schizophrenia at Home.* Kingston-upon-Thames: National Schizophrenia Fellowship (see under Useful Addresses).
This is the second edition of a book first published in 1974 and it clearly demonstrates that little changes for families trying to cope with serious mental illness. The first edition represented an innovative decision to reveal the experiences of relatives of sufferers and to present these in a 'plain and unvarnished way'. Two decades later the book is still a valuable source of information.

Howe, G. (1991) *The Reality of Schizophrenia.* London: Faber & Faber.
By the present author, this book sets out to explain the historical perspective and content of all the 'muddled thinking', as she puts it, surrounding schizophrenia. In doing this, it also covers most of the important aspects of coping with the illness.

Howe, G. (1997) *Serious Mental Illness: A Family Affair*. London: Sheldon Press.
This book, by the present author, is written to help lay-people understand conditions such as manic depression and schizophrenia. In particular, it is for sufferers and families trying to cope with this type of illness. It covers practical issues, getting the best from the system, coping in a crisis and, perhaps most importantly, how to avoid a crisis!

Howe, G. (1994) *Working with Schizophrenia: A Needs Based Approach*. London: Jessica Kingsley Publishers.
This book was written by the present author, with contributions from 12 sufferers and carers and several professional colleagues. Primarily written for individuals working with this illness, it has been warmly received in relevant professional journals.

Kuipers, L. and Bebbington, P. (1987) *Living With Mental Illness*. London: Souvenir Press Ltd. (Human Horizons Series).
This book was written by a psychologist and psychiatrist for relatives of the mentally ill and families should find it informative and helpful.

Manic Depression Fellowship (1995) *Inside Out: A Guide to Self Management of Manic Depression*. Produced and published by Manic Depression Fellowship (see under Useful Addresses).
This innovative and valuable booklet reflects the enthusiasm among the membership of MDF for a self-management approach to coping with this illness, largely inspired by the work of Mary Ellen Copeland (see above).

Manic Depression Fellowship (1997) *A Balancing Act*. Produced and published by Manic Depression Fellowship (see under Useful Addresses).
This booklet is to be published in Summer 1997. MDF's *Pendulum* reports it 'is aimed at the people who live alongside and help those who have a diagnosis of MD. It includes techniques and strategies which carers have found helpful.'

Varma, V. (1997) *Managing Manic Depressive Disorders*. London: Jessica Kingsley Publishers.

Useful addresses

Concern for the Mentally Ill
30 Arkwright Road
London NW3 6BH
Tel: 081 883 8533
A registered charity 'to promote and protect the welfare of the mentally disordered' and to provide a united voice for professionals involved in the care, treatment and rehabilitation of mentally vulnerable people'.

Depression Alliance
35 Westminster Bridge Road
London SE1 7JB
Tel: 0171 633 0557
Concerned with helping sufferers and their families to cope with a depressive illness. Provides advice and information about the illness and seeks to education public opinion. Regular newsletter, *A Single Step*.

Making Space
46 Allen Street
Warrington
Cheshire WA2 7JB
Tel: 0925 571680
Concerned with assisting sufferers and families in the North of England and promoting community care facilities and education.

Manic Depression Fellowship (MDF)
8–10 High Street
Kingston-upon-Thames
Surrey KT1 1EY
Tel: 0181–974 6550
Offers advice and support to those having to cope with MD, frequent open meetings and local self-help groups. Also involved in campaigning and promoting better services. Excellent quarterly journal, *Pendulum*.

National Schizophrenia Fellowship (NSF)
18 Castle Street
Kingston–upon–Thames
Surrey KT1 1SS
Tel: 0181–547 3937
Concerned with helping those affected by serious mental illness, while providing community services and promoting education and knowledge. Conferences and training days and local self–help groups throughout the country. Addresses and telephone numbers of regional offices can be obtained from head office. Quarterly newsletter, *NSF Today*.
Highly recommended helpline: 0181–547 6814 (10am – 3pm weekdays).

SANE
Concerned with research, campaigning and promoting knowledge about serious mental illness. Pioneering research at SANE's Prince of Wales International Centre in Oxford. Occasional newsletter, *Sanetalk*.
SANE Helpline: 0171–724 8000 (open afternoons, evenings and weekends).

Schizophrenia Association of Great Britain (SAGB)
International Schizophrenia Centre
Bryn Hyfryd
The Crescent
Bangor
Gwynedd LL57 2AG
Tel: 01248–354048
Involved in biochemical research into schizophrenia and helping sufferers and families to cope with schizophrenia. Occasional newsletter.

Subject Index

acceptance of
  diagnoses 20
access to information
  20, 21,123
  legal rights 24–5
acknowledgement of
  illness 11
  delays 12–14,
  118–19
adolescent psychiatric
  services see child
  psychiatric services
adolescent sufferers
  111–12,113–14,
  119,123
  Karen 107–9,
  112–13
  Kay 73–87
  Malcolm 58–72
age, and development
  of schizophrenia
  19, 25, 62, 68,70
ASWs (approved
  social workers) 65,
  127
Andrew's case 102
  training 38,40–1
awareness of diagnoses
  22

'bad behaviour'
  diagnoses 60,66

blaming parents 41,
  79–80,85
  Karen's case 108–9,
  111–12
  Kay's case 74
  Malcolm's case 66

care, duty to 65,70
'carers' definition 10
carers' group survey
  56
case studies 8–9
  Andrew 101–3
  Barry 43–57
  Jackie 15–27
  Jane 88–100
  Joan 104–6
  Karen 107–9
  Kay 73–87
  Malcolm 58–72
  Marie 28–42
  Naomi 103–4
  Ron 106–7
challenging
  diagnoses 36,
  38–9,40–1
child psychiatry
  services 78,119
  Kay's case 74,75,78
  Malcolm's case 59,
  63
Code of Practice
  (1993) 65, 70,85
comment sections 9
communication
  problems 115,
  121–2
  Barry's case 47–52,
  53–4, 55
community psychiatric
  nurses see CPNs

Concern for the
  Mentally Ill 132
continuity/co–ordinati
  on problems 115,
  121–2
  Barry's case 47–52,
  53–4,55
CPNs (community
  psychiatric nurses)
  127
  Barry's case 44,48
  Jane's case 88–9,90,
  95
  Joan's case 105
  training 38, 41,122

day centres, Barry's
  case 44–5, 50
day hospitals, Barry's
  case 44, 49
delays in
  acknowledgement
  of illness 12–14,
  118–19
  in diagnosis and
  treatment 67–9,
  71, 83,110,
  113,116–17
  in learning one's
  diagnosis 119–20
  in presenting
  physical
  symptoms only
  119
  young sufferers
  113–14
'delusion' definition
  127
'depot injections'
  definition 127

Depression Alliance 132
diabetes analogy 23,26
diagnoses 11
  acceptance of 20
  awareness of own 22
  challenging 36, 38–9, 40–1
  criteria 110, 115–16
  delays 67–9, 71,83, 110, 113,116–17
  'lack of' case study 28–42
  'precarious' 80–1
  rights to information 24–5,123
  'withholding' case study 15–27
Diagnostic and Statistical Manual of Mental Disorders 115
drug abuse 99
  case study 88,89, 93–4
duty to care 65,70

'edge of the system' case study 43–57
exercises 9
  individual cases 27, 41–2, 57, 72,87, 100, 117
explanations for families 11,22, 114,121–2

families
  Barry's case 46–7, 52,54–5
  'blaming' 41,66, 79–80,85
  informing 11,22, 114
  listening to 79,94–5
  Malcolm's case 59–60
  recognizing/ preventing relapses 11,97–8, 100,123
  support for 35, 56,81
  undervaluing 57,122
family theories 41, 79–80,127
family therapy
  Karen's case 107–8
  Malcolm's case 59, 63–4
feedback to professionals 52–3, 84,122–3
'first and only episodes 34,37,40, 123

genetic risks 128
GPs 53–4, 109–10, 120, 128
  Andrew's case 102
  Jane's case 88, 90, 95–6
  Joan's case 105
  Malcolm's case 59, 60, 62–3
  Ron's case 106,111
'hallucinations' definition 128

hospitalization 120
  Barry's case 44, 45–6, 49, 50–1
  Naomi's case 104
hostels, Barry's case 46, 51

information, access to 20, 21, 123
  legal rights 24–5
information sections 9
insight, sufferers' lack of 93

juvenile sufferers 111–12,113–14, 119,123
  Karen 107–9, 112–13
  Kay 73–87
  Malcolm 58–72

labelling 13, 20–2,33, 82
labelling theory 128
'lack of diagnosis' case study 28–42
law, mental health 64–5, 70, 82, 85, 120–1
LEAP group 7–8
legal rights, information access 24–5
listening to parents 79, 94–5

Making Space 132
manic depression 125–6

earlier diagnoses 69
Manic Depression
    Fellowship 132
medication,
    persevering with 26,
        34, 96–7,110–11
    Jackie's case 23
    Jane's case 89, 94
Mental Health Act
    64–5, 70, 85, 86,
    120–1
'mental health
    assessments'
    definition 128
monitoring, ongoing
    98

National Schizophrenia
    Fellowship 133
    surveys 71
'nearest relative'
    definition 128
neuroleptic medication
    128
'not knowing' case
    study 28–42
nursing training 38,41

occupational
    therapists 128
'one off' hopes 34,37,
    40,123
organizations, specialist
    24–5,26–7,122
    examples/addresses
        132–3

'paranoia' definition
    129
parents see families

personality disorders
    129
    Kay's case 76,80–1
    labelling 82
    treatability clause 86
physical symptoms,
    presenting 96,
    99,110,117,119
police, role of 71, 72,
    129
    Malcolm's case 61,
    66–7
'precarious' diagnoses
    80–1
professionals feedback
    to 52–3,84,122–3
    message for 10
    taking responsibility
        95–6
    training 38,
        40–1,122
    variations inapproach
        38, 39
    see also ASWs; CPNs;
        GPs; psychiatrists
psychiatric nurses129
    see also CPNs
psychiatrists 95–6,129
    Barry's case 45,
        48–9,50,51
    Jane's case 90,91,96
    Naomi's case 103–4
    Ron's case 106,111
'psychosis' definition
    129
psychotic episodes 11

quality disparities 121
questionnaires 8

referral baselines 124
relapses, recognizing
    and preventing 11,
    97–8,100,123
relatives see families
research project
    proposal, teenage
    sufferers 84
residential hospitals
    120
    Barry's case 45–6,
        50–1
    Naomi's case 104
responsibility issues 95

SAGB (Schizophrenia
    Association of
    Great Britain) 133
SANE 133
scapegoating see
    blaming parents
schizophrenia 126–7
    age of development
        19, 25, 62, 68,
        70
    diabetes analogy
        23,26
    stigma 20–1,33,37
Schizophrenia
    Association of
    Great Britain
    (SAGB) 133
sectioning 129
    grounds for
        64–5,70,82,85
self-management issues
    111,120
'serious mental illness'
    definition 11,129
service quality
    disparities 121

severity assessments 35
'slipping through the
    net', case studies
    72–87,88–100,
    114–15
social workers 65,
    127,129
Andrew's case 102
specialist organizations
    24–5,26–7,122
examples/addresses
    132–3
standardization of
    services 115–17
'staying in the system'
    see 'slipping
    through the net'
stigma fears 20–1,
    33,37
'sufferers' definition 10
'survivors' definition 10

teenage sufferers
    111–12,113–14,
    119,123
Karen 107–9,
    112–13
Kay 73–87
Malcolm 58–72
training, professional
    38,40–1,122
'treatability' clause
    82–3,86
treatment
case studies 101–17
    comment and
        analysis 109–13
    exercise 117
    wider perspectives
    67–71,113–17

need for early
    11,13
perils of delays
    68–9, 71, 83,
    116–17

voluntary
    organizations
    24–5, 26–7, 122
examples/addresses
    132–3

'ward round'
    situations 63
'withholding
    diagnosis' case study
    15–27

Name Index

All Saints Hospital, Birmingham 100
Andrew, treatment case study 101–3, 109, 112

Barry, 'edge of the system' case study 43–7
  comment/analysis 47–52, 120
  exercise 57
  wider perspectives 52–6
Birchwood, Max 100
Blakemore, Colin 85
Bleuler, M. 40

Coid, J. 86
Crow, T.J. 71, 116

Dexter, G. 41

Fuller, Torrey, E. 40

Howe, G. 13, 56, 85

Jackie, 'withheld diagnosis' case study 15–19
  comment/analysis 19–23, 119
  exercise 27
  wider perspectives 23–7

Jane, 'slipping through the net' case study 88–92
  comment/analysis 92–6, 114, 119, 120, 121, 122
  exercise 100
  wider perspectives 96–100
Joan, treatment case study 104–6, 109, 112
Johnstone, E.C. 12

Karen, treatment case study 107–9, 111–12, 112–13, 119
Kay, teenager case study 73–8
  comment/analysis 78–82, 119, 121
  exercise 87
  wider perspectives 82–6

Laing, R.D. 40–1

Malcolm, teenager case study 58–61
  comment/analysis 61–7, 119, 120, 121
  exercise 72
  wider perspectives 67–71

Marie, 'lack of diagnosis' case study 28–32
  comment/analysis 33–6, 114, 119–20
  exercise 41–2
  wider perspectives 37–41

Naomi, treatment case study 103–4, 109, 112

Ron, treatment case study 106–7, 110–11, 112, 119,120
Roth, M. 116

Slater, E. 116
Smith, Jo 100

Tyler, Mary 71

Wash, M. 41
Wyatt, R.J. 71, 116–17